William Henry

Incandescent electric lights

William Henry

Incandescent electric lights

ISBN/EAN: 9783337269524

Printed in Europe, USA, Canada, Australia, Japan

Cover: Foto ©Andreas Hilbeck / pixelio.de

More available books at **www.hansebooks.com**

NCANDESCENT

ELECTRIC

LIGHTS

With

Particular reference

to the

Edison lamps at the

Paris Exposition.

By

Th. du Moncel

and

Wm. Henry Preece.

New York
D. Van Nostrand
1882

PREFACE.

...successful experiments of
...maintaining a steady light of
...have become widely known,
...mber of systems have been
...ward by different inventors.
...e interest in the growth of
...tions affords a sufficient ex-
...of the appearance of an essay
...resent. The relative value of
...systems of lighting for interiors,
...pecially to economy of outfit
...nt power to maintain, will
...attention of all resi-

...w by Compte du
...international
...ays, re-
...EERING

MAGAZINE, one on "Economy of Electri
ghting," by Mr. Howell, of Steven
stitute, and another on "The Dynam
ectric Current," by Dr. C. Willian
emens. and a third by W. H. Preec
. the results of the Paris Exhibition.

INCANDESCENT ELECTRIC LAMPS.

EDISON'S SYSTEM OF ELECTRIC LIGHTING.

THE incandescent system was first rep-
nted by lamps made from an incan-
ent platinum wire, and the interest-
experiments made in 1879 by M. de
Angy, should be recollected ; but the
actical workings of this system were not
atisfactory, principally because of the dis-
ggreration and partial fusion of the wires,
and in spite of the numerous improve-
ment brought to bear on this system by
Edison, who, by one of the most in-
of processes, had rendered them
rfusible and harder, still they had
absolutely rejected—at least for or-
y lamps. Then it was suggested to
oy carbon which, if not allowed to
.., is infusible if the highest heat de-
ped in the lamps, and different ar-
ements of apparatus were put to-
at various times by King, Lody-
e, Bouliguin, Swan, Sawyer, etc.,

some avoiding combustion
the lamps in receptacles where
had been obtained, others by fillin,
receptacles with gases unfit for comb
tion. as nytrogen or oxide of carbon,
simply by leaving the air shut up in t
receptacle to be vitiated by an incipi
combustion.

All these attempts had but part
succeeded, to say nothing more, w
in 1879, the new incandescent car
lamp of Mr. Edison was announced, an
many savants, and myself in particular
doubted the exactness of the allegation
which came to us from America. The
carbonized paper horse shoe appeared
incapable of resisting mechanical shock,
and of supporting incandescence for any
length of time. At this epoch Mr. Swan
himself said that up to that time he
had not been able to obtain any very
satisfactory results by an analagous disposition of the incandescent organ.

Mr. Edison, however, was not abashed
and in spite of the lively opposition made
to his lamps, in spite of the bitter po

lemic of which he was the object, he did
not cease to perfect it for practical purposes, and has at last produced lamps,
which we have seen at the Exposition,
and which can be admired by all the
world for their perfect steadiness. These
lamps. to the number of 160, light the
two salons reserved for the discoveries
of the ingenious American inventor, and
we shall see still more important results
upon the installation of the great machine which is expected from America.

As at present made, these lamps are
sufficiently solid and can last a long time.
The originally fragile carbon has become
extremely elastic and hard, and of such
attenuation that it can be well compared
in size to a horse hair. By a cleverly
combined system of fastening the platinum. conducting wires are not exposed
to be cut, and they are so sealed in the
glass receiver that their change of vol-
ume under the action of heat does not
endanger the perfection of th vacuum.
By the way the carbons are treated when
the vacuum is made in the globe, the

bubbles of air enclosed in their pores and which, in escaping, disaggregate the surface, are evacuated before closing the lamp, and at the same time the filament of carbon acquires a peculiar density and hardness, as was the case with the platinum wires. To obtain this result the carbonized filament must be brought into incandescense while the vacuum is being made. The very nature of the substance of vegetable origin employed in its fabrication, has been modified.

Fibers of bamboo are now used instead of the paper originally employed. These are carbonized by a certain process, and the successive transformation of these fibers into carbon filaments may be followed in several collections to be seen at Mr. Edison's exposition, and which will gratify the curious, and are worthy of study. According to Mr. Batchelor and Mr. O. A. Moses, co-laborers of Mr. Edison, and who represent him at the exposition, the resistance of these filaments is 125 ohm, when brought up to an incandescence corresponding to 16 candles;

but it can vary according to the luminous power desired of the lamps, for it can be distributed between two lamps, whose filaments are correspondingly more or

Fig. I.   **Fig. 2.**

less long. Their extremities, which are enlarged, are pressed in a kind of pincer which terminates the platinum conductors, and which are soldered by an electrolytically deposited copper. Figs. 1, 2, 3

and 4 represents the actual arrangement
of these lamps. Their duration, from what
I have been assured, is long enough;

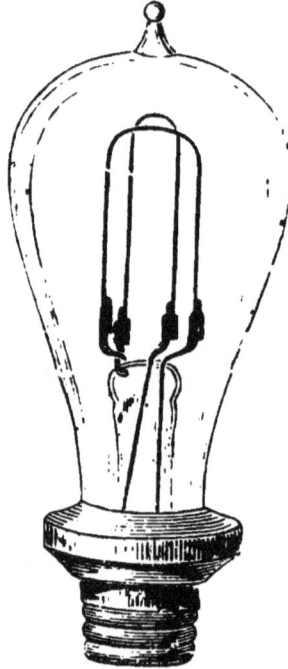

Fig. 3.

however, they must wear out. Although
most of them may have served for 1,200
hours, the question may be asked,whether
a lamp capable of deterioration may be

considered a practical thing ; but if it is
considered that this lamp can be furnished for 30 cents, that the adjustment

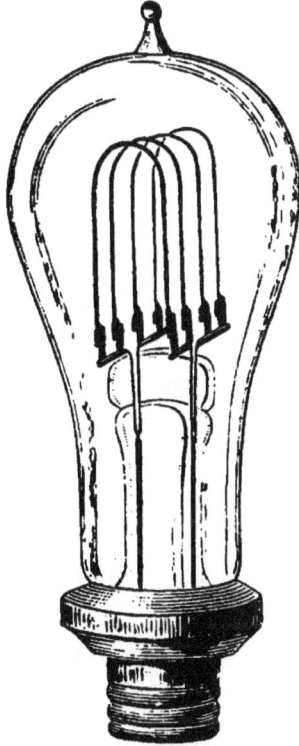

Fig. 4.

on its support cannot be any simpler than
it is. which is evident on inspection, it is
easily seen there is no more trouble to

replace one than to renew a broken lamp shade.

What constitutes Mr. Edison's system is not alone his lamps, it is the totality of the arragements referring to them and which have attained such a degree of simplicity that henceforth nothing remains to be desired in practice. Generating machines, distribution of circuits, installation, indicating and regulating apparatus, meters for measuring the amount of current employed are all combined for immediate application. As we have said, this application is about being made in a part of the city of New York, where a great number of houses are to be lighted by this system, by means of a subterranean distribution from a central station, from which also motive power will be distributed to the houses.

This central station will be provided with twelve steam engines of 150 horse power each, actuating dynamo-electric machines, each of which will be capable to supply, it is said, 2,400 lamps of 8

candle power. The current furnished
to these lamps comes through a branch
taken before each house from the large-
sized conductors laid in the streets.
These deviations bring the poles of the
generator into each house, where the
lamp wires can be brought in connection
with them, thus rendering each house
independent of any other, both for a
supply of light and motive power.

When it is considered that the system
of distribution adopted by Mr. Edison,
the total resistance of the exterior circuit is extremely reduced and that with
2,400 lamps it is only $\frac{64}{2\,400}$, say, about
.026 of an ohm, it can be seen that a very
feeble resistance should be given to the
generating machine ; so that its first arrangement has been modified. To begin
with: The field magnets were arranged on
a derivation taken from the commutator,
putting it into the induced circuit as in
Wheatstone's and Siemens' system.
Then the armature was arranged on Siemens' principle, so that the wire con-

sisted of bars of copper. These bars lie close to each other around the cylinder which forms the armature, and they generate the current. Their extremities correspond to discs of copper (at right angles to them) laid one against the other at the ends of the cylinder, and insulated from each other. Each bar is fastened to its corresponding discs in such a way as to form a single circuit enveloping the cylinder longitudinally, and which is made perfect through the coupled bars two and two with the commutator blocks (made after the Grammes pattern). Figs. 5 and 6 give an idea of this new arrangement. The center of the cylinder itself is occupied outside of the rotating axle by a cylinder of wood, which, in its turn, is surrounded by a thick tube made of a series of very thin discs of iron, separated from each other by tissue paper. This arrangement facilitates the rapid changes of polarity in the plates. This tube is terminated at its two extremities by two thick clamping discs which are made to compress the others

laterally, and the copper discs of the
working coil occupy the two compart-

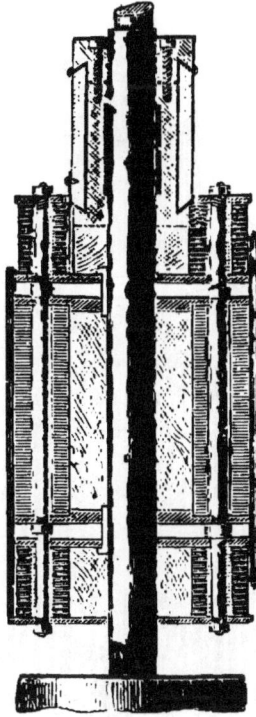

Fig. 5.

ments at the extremities of the cylinder,
as seen in Fig. 5. Under such conditions as these the resistance of the gene-

rator is small, and permits of great sub-
division of the current in multiple arc;

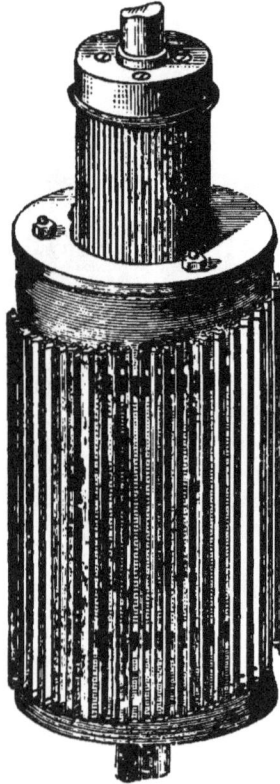

Fig. 6.

nor is there any insulation to be burned,
and it is even possible, in case of the
deterioration of the bars, to renew them

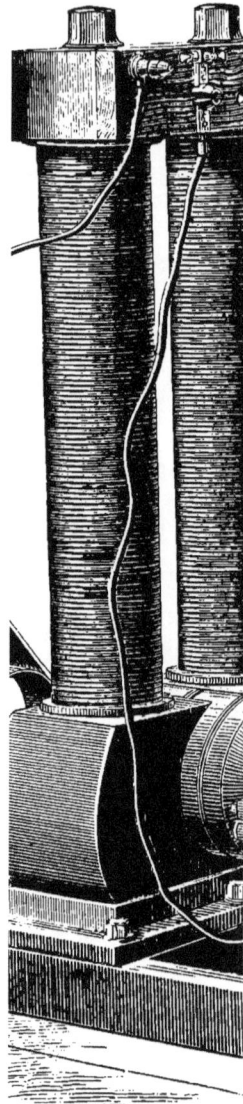

Fig. 7.

easily, for they are simply screwed against the copper discs corresponding to them. In the new disposition adopted by Mr. Edison, the field magnets lie horizontal instead of being placed in the vertical.

Fig. 7 represents the whole machine as now actually working in the Palais de l'Industrie.

We have described the generating machine before completing the description of the system of distribution of the current, because we ought to speak of the system of control used in making the current uniform when its intensity has been modified by a variation in its distribution; that is to say, following after a variation resulting from the unexpected suppression of a certain number of lamps in a part of the system. The necessities of this system are easily understood, if we consider that this suppression can lead to a greater or less increase in the intensity of the current feeding the remaining lamps.

In France several systems have been devised to obtain an automatic regulation, but in America, it seems, it is preferred to effect this by the intermediation of an appropriate controlling agent.

In this system, in whose general arrangement we see, in Fig. 8, the current which feeds the lamps furnishes a deviation at the machine cc, which enters an electric dynamometer, after having gone through a resistance of 180,000 ohms. The electro-motive force should be about 110 volts, and a difference of one volt should correspond on the scale of the indicating apparatus to three divisions; consequently, for each observed increase of intensity a resistance capable of compensating for it should be introduced into the circuit. Mr. Edison has established a circular commutator e with bobbins of different resistance, which permits of an increase of resistance, not in the lamp circuit, which would lead to a loss of work, but in the circuit of field magnets, which weakens their action on the working coil. From the central station also, the condition of the current affecting the lamps can be controlled by means of

364.58

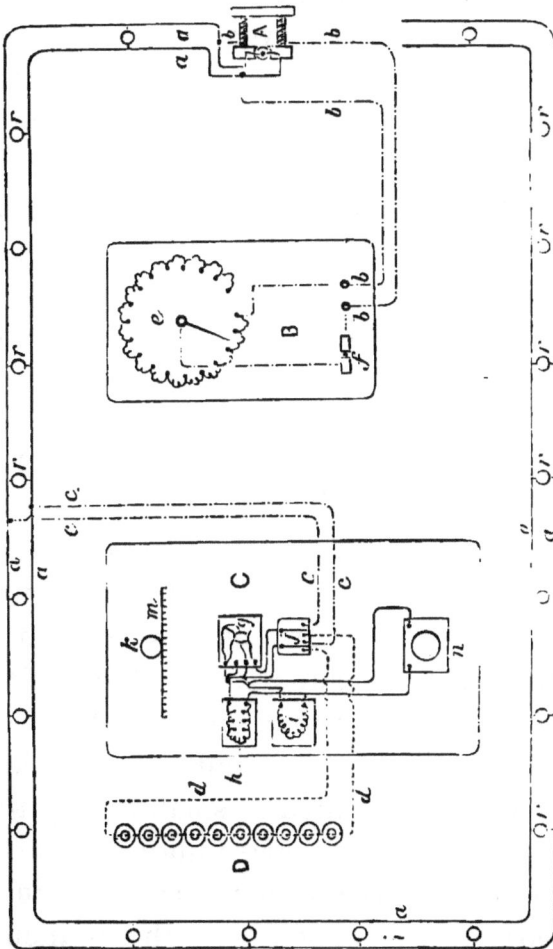

Fig. 8.

a testing photometer, which enables us to
see how much the intensity of the current must be diminished or increased to
correspond to a given luminous intensity. For this purpose the photometer is
mounted on a little railroad, placed in a
dark chamber ; under and in front of it
is placed a scale, arbitrarily divided, so
as to indicate immediately the candle
power furnished by the current in its
normal condition. The left side of Fig. 8
indicates the manner of arrangement of
the testing bench, with the explanatory
table at the bottom of the figure. Fig. 9
shows it in perspective. The manner in
which derivations are taken on the principal conductors merits especial mention.
The conductors are composed of two rods
of copper of hemi-cylindrical form, flat on
one side and round on the other, which
are enveloped in cylinders of insulating
material, contained in small wrought-iron
pipes, which are buried under the streets.
To take a derivation the cable is laid
bare at the spot where the branch circuit is to be established. The two con.

Fig. 9.

ducting rods (coming from the main co⌐
ductors) are cut and bent outwards ar⌐
introduced into a clamp where they a⌐

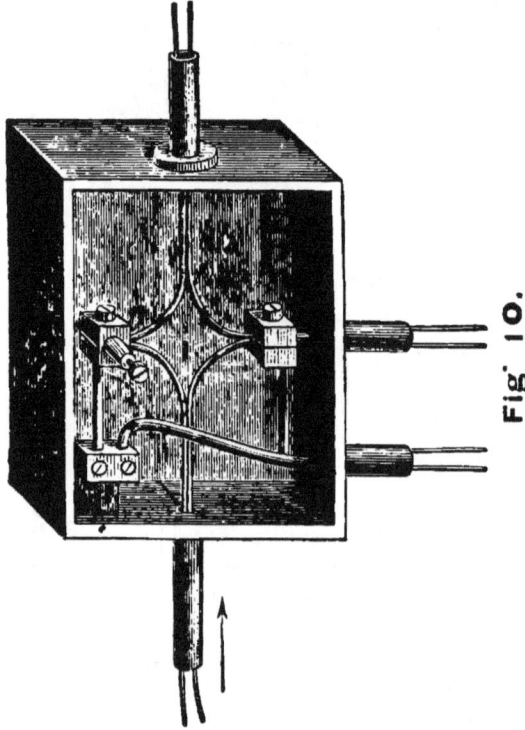

Fig. 10.

soldered to the house wires, as shown in
Fig. 10; but in order that no harm can be
done by two strong currents, one of these
communications is made by intercalating

a lead wire in the branch circuit, shown at the bottom of the figure, and which, by its fusion, interrupts the circuit. This is what is called in America a "cut off;" and in this way it prevents deterioration. The box is then hermetically closed and covered with an insulating coating. In the figure the branch wires are shown double, but it is evident that they could b e single.

We said that all arrangements had been made to make the system a perfectly practical one, and of that we will soon be able to judge. Let us examine first how the lamp supports and the lamps themselves are disposed. As has been seen, they are formed of glass globes of ovoid form, cemented into copper sleeves by means of plaster and screwed into cylindrical cavities terminating the supports. These are a kind of arm which can be adapted to brackets or chandeliers, or be arranged around the walls. In the last case, the arm, as is shown in Fig. 11, carry two articulations, A and B, and commutations are made by two plates of the hinges

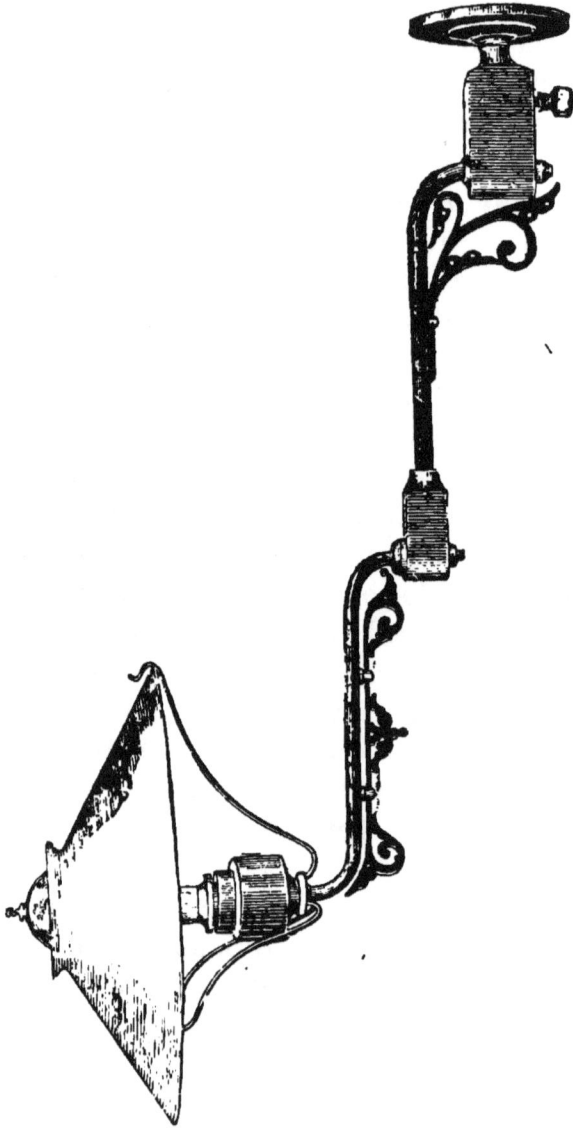

Fig. 11.

which are insulated, and in whose circular part two springs press, as seen in Figs. 12 and 13. Connections of the con-

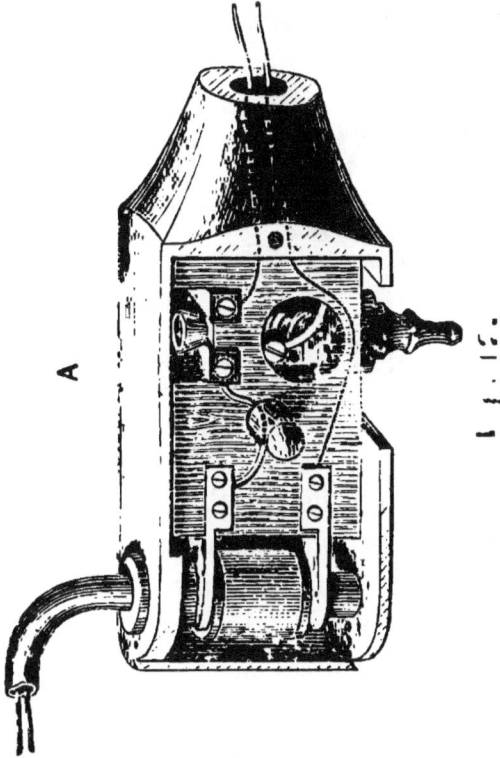

A

Fig. 13.

ductors with the lamp, as we have indicated above, are made by a lead wire (cut off) which may melt and interrupt the

circuit in case a too great quantity of
current should endanger the lamp.

In these brackets, as in the three
branch chandeliers, represented in Fig.
14, keys have been introduced which
allow the extinction of the lamps separ-

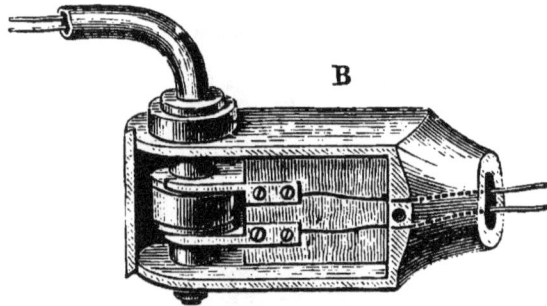

Fig. 13.

ately or together, without causing any
spark of the point of rupture or any danger of fire. The movement of the key a,
as shown in Fig. 12, breaks the contact by
means of a conical stopper which terminates the screw of the key, and which,
when separated from the two plates,
through which the current passes when
the stopper is in contact with them,

breaks the circuits at the points and on
a surface of sufficient extent to greatly
diminish the spark at the point of rupture.

Fig. 14.

The lighting of the two salons of Mr.
Edison at the Exposition is done by 16
small chandeliers like the above, two
grand crystal chandeliers and 80 brackets.

The effect is very beautiful, the steadiness being as complete as could be desired, and if, as I have been assured, the price of this kind of illumination is lower, light for light, than gas, it may be considered that the problem is on the eve of solution, for Edison's system of electric lighting is placed in the same condition as that of gas. He avoids the presence of machines in separate houses, which always are in the way, and which, by their very nature, require care and management not to be obtained from ordinary servants.

As a complement to his system, Mr. Edison has constructed portable chandeliers, represented in Fig. 15, and a current regulator shown in Figures 16 and 17, which permits of reducing the light in any desired proportion. It is a carbon rheostat, composed of carbon pencils of different sections, which, as the current passes through one or the other, allows any desired intensity. The apparatus is enveloped in a cylindrical cover, pierced with holes to allow of the escape

of heat, and surmounted by a lamp
which indicates to the eye the desired degree of luminacy. It is worked by a

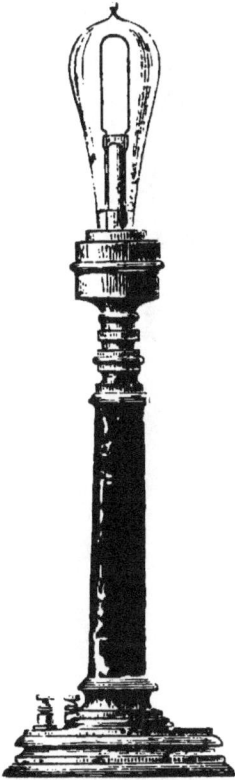

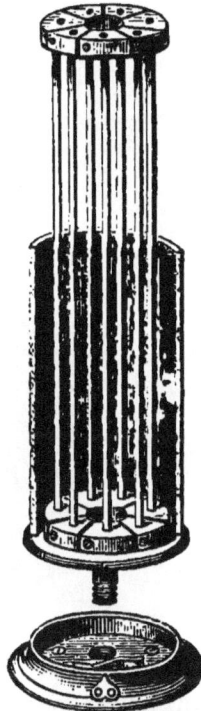

Fig. 15.   **Fig. 16.**

disc, shown separated in the lower part
of Fig. 16, and which can be turned so
as to bring a contact spring on any one

of the supports of the carbon, whose
position is indicated by an index and divisions engraved on the base of the
cylinder.

Fig. 17.

But what is most interesting of all in
those accessories of Mr. Edison's system, is the meter which determines the
amount of electricity consumed by the

lamps. There are two kinds, one automatic like a gas meter, the other requires weighing. They are, however, both founded on the same principle, that is to say, in the estimation of work by the weight of a copper deposit produced by the current used. We will describe these two interesting pieces of apparatus hereafter, and give drawings of them; to-day we must be content with only mentioning the principle involved.

Imagine a balance having at the extremities of the beam two cylindrically rolled plates of copper forming two electrodes. Let us admit that these two systems of electrodes, which plunge into two vessels filled with a solution of sulphate of copper and furnished with fixed electrodes, are traversed in an inverse direction by the current employed, and which can cause the balance to operate under a given weight of copper deposited from the solution. It is easily seen that the movement brought about by these conditions can set in motion a current reverser, which can change the conditions of the deposits in such a way that the electrode. covered with copper, is transformed into a soluble electrode. while the one which was originally in that condition becomes the reducing electrode. From this time on an oscillating motion of the beam of the balance is established. and more or less frequently repeated, according to the rapidity of the formation of deposit. that is to say, according to the intensity of the current. As the same movement can bring about the passage of a derived current (taken from the total current) across a special electro-magnet, which commands the movement of a counter. it is easily seen (after the determination of the number of Amperes corresponding to the weight of the deposit, which produces the oscillation of the balance) what is the quantity of electricity consumed.

The realization of this idea has necessitated some electro-magnetic arrangements, which we will describe in detail when we get the drawings of the apparatus.

The other system is more simple, con-
sisting of two voltameters of sulphate
of copper, whose electrodes can be easily
taken out and weighed, as the work done
can be calculated from the weight of
copper deposited. One of these voltameters is open to the subscriber, the other
is kept closed by the controller. Resist
ance bobbins introduced into the circuit
corresponding to these resistance, permits of the employment of greater or
less periods of registration.

A small incandescent lamp placed be-
neath the apparatus, and which can be
thrown into circuit by a simple metallic
thermometer, prevents any danger of
freezing in extremely cold weather.

There is another application of Mr.
Edison's light, which can be seen at his
exposition in a model intended for lighting galleries in mines. In this arrangement, represented in Fig. 18, the lamp is
introduced in a glass receptacle filled
with water and held in suspension.
Communication of the apparatus with
the circuit is arranged in such a way

that the points of contact are covered by
water, which avoids any danger of ex-
plosion in mines infested with fire damp.

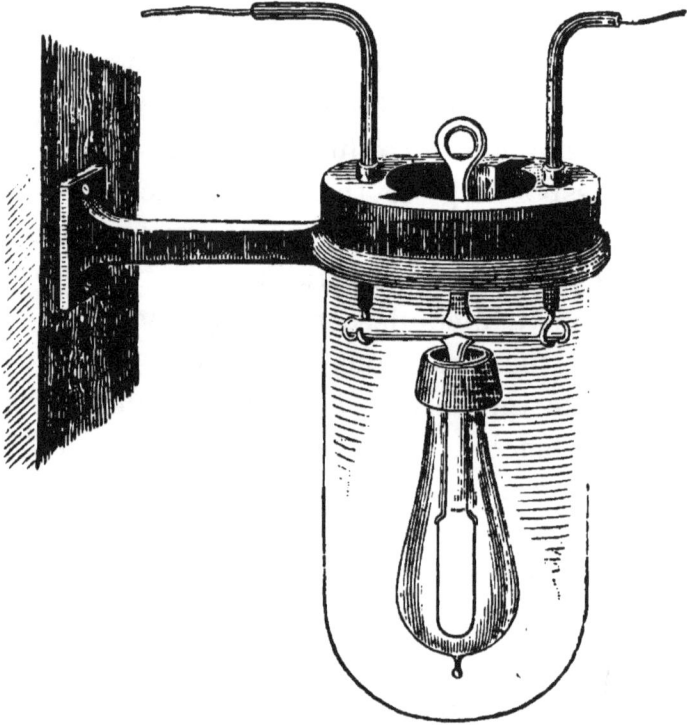

Fig. 18.

To give an idea of the application of
Mr. Edison's systems, we have represented in the large engraving accompanying
this article, Fig. 19, the interior of a

parlor lighted by the small chandeliers previously described. As is seen, the electric light is projected downward, the best arrangement for reading and writing. This method seems to be preferred by Mr. Edison, but as can be seen above described that all styles of illumination can be produced with this kind of light, analogous to that obtained with candles or gas jets, it is simply a matter of taste.

Mr. Edison's lamps are not alone employed in the two salons reserved for him, they are to be found in various places throughout the great nave, notably at the exhibits of Messrs. Heilman, Ducommun et Stienben (of which we gave a drawing in a previous article) and at the exhibit of Messrs. Sautter and Lemonnier. At these two places the currents are furnished by two Gramme machines, type A, and each one lights about 40 lamps. Now that Mr. Edison's great machine (a drawing of which is shown on frontispiece) has arrived at the Exposition, it will be possible to ob-

Fig. 19.

tain, with the incandescent system, illu-
minations of greater magnitude. The
landing of the great staircase will be lit
in this way. It is proposed to accom-
plish this by means of a crystal chande-
lier of 144 lamps, and of others furnished with 25 lamps each, to be hung from
the different panels, and of girandoles
standing on the 16 pilasters of the staircase. This will produce an enchanting
effect and a brilliant illumination. I am
not quite sure that this mixture of arc
and incandescent lights is a happy
thought. It is evident that the latter
destroy the effect of the former, and
might lead one to believe that the luminous intensity of the incandescent lamp is
less than it really is. Again, the difference in the color of the lights is so con-
trasted that many persons who reproach
the electric for its ghastly aspect, find it
too red in incandescent lamps. It is
evidently an effect of contrast, for the
light of incandescent lamps is whiter
than that of gas jets, which, neverthe-
less, these same people find very agreea-

ble. If required, incandescent lamps can give a dazzling white just as well as the others; it is only necessary to employ a stronger electrical intensity, then they lose their peculiar qualities, that of giving a soft light which does not fatigue the eye and of an easier and more complete subdivion.

It is certainly very difficult to satisfy everybody, and that many persons hardly know what they do want: above all, when the effects of contrast momentarily impair the power of judging correctly. On the other hand, there are certain fault-finding spirits who are never satisfied with anything; witness the author of that incomprehensible article that recently appeared in a certain journal, who pretended that only discordant sounds and puppet-show voices could be heard in the telephones from the opera. The author in question who could perpetrate such an enormity must have had his ear as sick as his humor. The crowd passing every evening before the telephone rooms at the Exposition, is the best proof of the inanity

of such judgments, and by this can once
more be seen the value of the scientific
lucubrations of certain political journals.
The same thing happens with the electric light, and quite a number of persons
who, without previous examination, and
without being of the same opinion two
days consecutively, come to us and disparage electric lighting. It is certain
that new inventions have great difficulty
in coming to light and in succeeding,
above all when they are opposed by rival
interests, but when they are really good
they triumph in time over all obstacles.

We would like to give some information about Mr. Edison's new machines,
but as they are not yet put up we re-
serve the description for another time;
we will only say that the steam engine
was constructed especially for this application, that it makes no noise, and that
the dynamo-electric machine forms one
of its integral parts. The field magnets
of this latter-mentioned, in place of being vertical as in the model represented
in Fig. 7, is horizontal, and the dimen-

sions of the machine itself are much larger.

The steam engine, which works the machine, is of peculiar construction, and the speed of rotation which is communicated to the working coil is 350 turns a minute. This is not a very great speed, but the armature is very heavy, weighing, as we are told, over three tons and a half. The magnetic field in which it turns is formed by three powerful electro-magets, united so as to form but one at their extremities. In the salon of Mr. Edison are a collection of photographs, among which may be seen some of the manufactures where the enormous amount of material required in these installations is constructed. As we have been assured, one of these turns out 2,000 lamps a day, giving occupation to 150 persons. In accompanying drawings and collections can be seen methods of glass blowing, the carbonizing of the filaments intended for incandescence, the vacuum pumps and the mounting and packing of the lamps. The pumps referred to are set in motion by dynamo-electric machines.

From all this, we see Mr. Edison's system to-day is completed, perfectly studied out in all its parts, and that nothing more remains to be done, but to introduce it on a great scale.

Th. Du Moncel.

[Note by the Translator.]

DESCRIPTION OF EDISON'S STEAM DYNAMO.

(*See Frontispiece.*)

Peculiar to the Edison system is the idea of connecting an engine of great power directly to the armature shaft of a single dynamo, capable of absorbing the full power of the engine, and of economically converting the same into electrical energy for distribution to the lamps and motors. To obtain the requisite electrical pressure, and avoid the use of magnets and armature of a weight and size which for mechanical and commercial reasons would be excessive, the engine is so constructed as to maintain a speed of 350 revolutions. A boiler pressure of 120 lbs., made absolutely safe by the use of approved sectional boilers, the high speed, and variable cut-off valve, and manner of constructing the engine makes this method of generating electricity absolutely safe and economical, and the uniformity obtained in regulation of speed insures a corresponding steadiness in the current and therefore in the lights which it supplies.

The following approximate summary of weights and dimensions of various parts of the latest "steam dynamo" constructed will give an idea of its total size and power.

Cast-iron sole plate, in one piece, upon which dynamo and engine are placed, and pillow blocks, 9,600 lbs.; Magnets, complete, 24,500 lbs.; Armature, complete, and shaft, 8,500 lbs.; Engine, 10,000 lbs. Total weight, 44,600 lbs.

The total weight of copper on armature and magnets is 3,600 lbs.

Principal dimensions: Sole plate $12\frac{1}{2}$ × $8\frac{1}{2}$ ft.; length of magnets, 8 ft.;

length of armature (commutator makes additional length of 9″) 5ft.; diameter of armature, 28″; Engine cylinder, 11″ × 16″; capacity, 2,400 gas jets.

ECONOMY

OF

ELECTRIC LIGHTING

BY

INCANDESCENCE.

By JOHN W. HOWELL.

STEVENS' INSTITUTE OF TECHNOLOGY.

I.—ECONOMY OF THE GENERATOR.
II.—ECONOMY OF THE CONDUCTOR.
III.—ECONOMY OF THE LAMPS.

Economy of Electric Lighting by Incandescence.

In writing this thesis I have endeavored to determine as nearly as I was able the cost of electric lighting by incandescence. Owing to the interest attached to the subject, and the lack of data upon which calculations can be based, I have endeavored to consider the subject in all its details, and have taken every precaution that suggested itself to guard against error.

The data given are sufficient to calculate the number of lamps to be obtained from each indicated horse power in a steam engine; beyond this I have not attempted to go, as my experience is insufficient to enable me to make any further determinations.

EFFICIENCY OF THE GENERATOR.

The generator tested was one of the latest pattern devised by Mr. Edison. It

differs from the generators heretofore in
general use, principally in the substitution
of bars of copper for wires in the armature,
which make the resistance of the armature
very low and also economizes space, as the
bars have a trapezoidal section, and when
in position there is only clearance enough
to allow for the insulation between them.

In my experiments the field was excited
by a current shunted from the main circuit, the relative resistances of the mains
and magnet coils determining the amount
of energy expended on the magnets, and
consequently the intensity of the magnet-
ization and the electro-motive force of
the generator.

APPARATUS FOR MEASUREMENT OF THE ME-
CHANICAL ENERGY TRANSMITTED TO THE
GENERATOR.

In measuring the energy transmitted to
the generator, the dynamometer built by
the class of '79 was used. This was carefully standardized by supporting the pendulum in a horizontal position at a point
2 feet from the axis of the shaft, and

weighing the pressure of the support upon a platform scale ; the weight of the pendulum and support was 183.25; the weight of the support was 12.1 ; the weight of the pendulum was 171.2 lbs.

This gives us the force acting at the circumference of a pulley of 1 foot radius by multiplying 171.2 by the sine of the angle of deflection. This is a measure of the force transmitted through the gear at the top of the pendulum, and includes, beside the force required to turn the armature in the field of force, the force necessary to overcome the friction of the dynamometer bearing, and also the friction of the armature shaft in its bearings. In order to determine what part of the transmitted energy was lost in overcoming friction, a Prony brake was applied to the pulley of the armature, close beside the belt, while the generator was running. Removing the brushes to be sure no current was generated, we tightened the brake until the pendulum showed the same deflection that it did during the test : we thus made a direct substitution of the Prony brake for the retarding action of the lines of magnetic force upon the armature when the circuit was closed, and the force exerted by the arm of the brake, upon a platform scale reduced to the radius of the pulley, will be the force required to turn the armature in the field of force. Instead of measuring the pressure exerted by one arm of the brake upon a scale, we measured the lifting effort exerted by the other end upon a weight resting upon the scale. We placed a light counterweight upon the other end of the brake, to make the zero reading more definite, and in getting the zero we raised the counterweighted end, and let it down gently, rapping the center of the brake to prevent sticking.

Several readings fixed the zero between $35\frac{1}{2}$ and 35. Running at about the same speed as in the test, and tightening the brake until we got a deflection of $42°$, we made several readings on the scale, which varied from 19 to $20\frac{1}{2}$. Using the highest zero reading and the lowest running reading, we get a force of $16\frac{1}{2}$ lbs. acting at a distance of 2 feet from the center of the shaft; this reduced to the radius of the armature pulley gives $16\frac{1}{2} \times \frac{24}{5} = 79.2$ for the force acting at the circumference of the armature pulley. If no friction had intervened this force would have been

$$\frac{171.2 \times (\text{sine } 42° = 66.913)}{125} = 91.644 \text{ lbs.,}$$

showing a loss of $91.644 - 79.2 = 12.444$ lbs., or $13\frac{1}{2}$ per cent. of the power transmitted.

This loss of $13\frac{1}{2}$ per cent. is caused by the friction of the dynamometer and the friction of the armature bearings. To get the force actually applied at the circumference of the pulley on the armature shaft, we must determine the friction of the dynamometer bearing alone. To do this we made a wooden brake of the same diameter as the driving pulley on the dynamometer that could run on a 10-inch pulley on the dynamometer shaft, we then clamped the Prony brake upon the dynamo pulley, and also clamped the belt on the dynamo pulley and passed it over the

wooden brake. Running under these conditions and tightening the wooden brake
on the 10-inch pulley until the pendulum
showed a deflection of 42°, we measured
the force acting at the circumference of
the dynamo pulley and also at the circumference of the dynamometer pulley by the
lifting effort of the Prony brake upon the
weight on the scale. The object of this
arrangement of brakes was to get the
friction under the same conditions as
those under which we ran the test. To
get the zero reading in this case we
clamped the Prony on the dynamo pulley,
and loosened the wooden brake and counterweighted the other arm of the Prony
brake, until the armature turned in its
bearings; then letting it come to rest and
rapping the bearings of the dynamo and
dynamometer, we determined the zero
reading to be 33 lbs. Several readings
fixed the readings for 42° at 16 lbs.,
therefore the force acting at the circumference of the dynamo pulley was (33—16)

$\times \dfrac{24}{5} = 81.6$, showing a loss of 91.644—81.6

=10.044 lbs., or 10.9 per cent. of the total energy transmitted.

APPARATUS FOR THE MEASUREMENT OF ELECTRICAL ENERGY.

The resistance over which the generator worked consisted of three strands of iron wire in multiple arc, each of which was .104″ in diameter. These were stretched from one gallery of the shop to the other in the open air.

In measuring the resistance of the different parts of the circuit wires were led from the binding posts of the generator to the Wheatstone bridge, then by breaking the connection with the armature and magnet coils, we could measure the resistance of the line, or by breaking the connections with the line and magnets we could measure the resistance of the armature and leaders, or by breaking the connections with the armature and the line we could measure the resistance of the magnet coils.

The electrical energy developed in the circuit was determined by three methods:

1st. By a voltameter, or a copper-depositing cell.

2d. By a calorimeter.

3d. By measuring the electro-motive force and resistance.

FIRST METHOD.

The voltameter consisted of a glass jar large enough to hold six plates of copper, $7'' \times 8''$.

These were placed $\frac{1}{2}''$ apart, and held in place by a light wooden frame. They were connected alternately to the positive and negative wires from the generator. This method of arranging the plates brings both sides into action, gives a large area of plate, and makes the resistance of the cell very low and the consequent heating very little. By means of mercury connections the voltameter could be thrown into or out of circuit instantly without breaking the current, and the leaders were so proportioned that throwing it in and out did not alter the resistance of the circuit.

In calculating the current from the

weight of copper carried from one set of plates to the other, the weight gained by the negative plates was considered as the weight carried over, and the constant .32456, given by Sprague (Jenkin gives .324) for the amount of copper in milligrams carried over in one second by a current of one Weber. Before making the test, the current was passed through the voltameter for some time, in a direction opposite to that in which it was passed during the test, to insure that the copper carried over during the test was copper that had been deposited before, otherwise energy may be lost in separating the copper from the positive plate.

SECOND METHOD.

In determining the electrical energy by the second method, a calorimeter was used which consisted of a cylindrical vessel of galvanized iron encased in a wooden jacket, and so supported as to leave an air space of about $\frac{1}{2}$ an inch on all sides between the calorimeter and the jacket. This prevented any great conduction of heat from the calorimeter to external objects; still some heat must be wasted in heating the calorimeter and the surface it rests upon.

To determine the amount of heat thus wasted 55 lbs of water was put in the calorimeter, and its temperature carefully determined it was 19.85°C. A large pail of water was then heated to 54.3°C, and $18\frac{3}{4}$ lbs. were poured into the calorimeter. This made the weight of water in the calorimeter about the same as was used in the test, and the same part of the calorimeter was heated in each case, the final temperature of the water being 28.50°C, the range of temperature used in the test was included in this range. The heat contained in the water poured into the calorimeter may be represented by $18.75 \times 26.2 = 491.25$. Of this $55 \times 8.65 = 475.75$ went to raise the temperature of the water in the calorimeter, and the remainder 155 must have been imparted to the calorimeter. As the range of temperature in the calorimeter was 8.65°, 1.78 of these units were required to raise the temperature 1°, or the same amount of heat was used in heating the calorimeter as would be re-required to raise 1.78 lbs. of water through the same range of temperature; therefore the proper correction may be applied by adding 1.78 lbs. to the weight of water in the calorimeter.

To measure the heating effect of the current, a coil of copper wire was put into the calorimeter, the resistance of which was exactly $.1\frac{1}{10}$ Ohm, at 74° F. The chief source of error in a calorimeter test of this kind is the tendency of the current to pass from one part of the wire to another through the water, instead of passing through the wire. This in itself is not a source of error if we measure the resistance of the coil in the water, but in so passing, it may carry metal from one part of the wire to another, and the energy so used cannot be calculated, and is lost ; to obviate this difficulty distilled water was used, the resistance of which is much higher than ordinary water. The resistance of the coil measured in the water did not differ perceptibly from its resistance in the air, and at the close of the test no evidence of copper having been carried from one part to the other was discernable. To determine the range of temperature during the test. a Fahrenheit thermometer was used that was graduated to fifths of degrees. but the graduation was so plain that twentieths of a degree could easily be read. In order to be certain that the temperature of the water was uniform throughout a pump was placed in the center of the calorimeter. which consisted simply of a copper tube about $1\frac{3}{4}''$ in diameter. its bottom was $\frac{1}{4}''$ above the bottom of the calorimeter and contained a valve opening downward : the piston also carried a valve opening downward. The water in the calorimeter covered the top of the tube, and by this means the water was taken from the surface when it is warmest. and carried to the bottom, where it is coldest. The circulation thus obtained was very perfect, as shown by some ink drops put in the pump barrel.

THIRD METHOD.

In determining the electrical energy by the third method. the electro-motive force was measured between the binding posts of the generator, by means of a Thomson high-resistance galvanometer. As a standard of electro-motive force, Latimer Clark cells were used, four of which were made up new for the purpose. These agreed with each other very closely, and in using them they were connected in series, thus getting their combined effect, and averaging their errors.

In using them they were allowed to charge a condenser, and the condenser was then discharged through the galvanometer.

The deflection produced is an accurate measure of the current flowing through the galvanometer and consequently of the charge held by the condenser, which depends upon the electro-motive force of the terminals connected with the condenser. To connect the condenser alternately with the cells and the galvanometer, a simple switch was used by which the change could be made instantly. In making the test part of the condenser of $.2\frac{2}{10}$ microfarad capacity wire used and four standard cells in series. The damping magnet of the galvanometer was then adjusted until the discharge of the condenser produced a deflection of 291 divisions, as the electromotive force of the cell is 1,456 volts and four in series were used, the deflection corresponding to one volt was $\dfrac{291}{1.456 \times 4}$ $=50$. The instrument being standarized, in this way, the liability to error was very small ; in use, however, $\frac{9}{10}$ of the current was shunted from the galvanometer, only allowing $\frac{1}{10}$ to pass through, thus getting five deflections to a volt.

The ends of all wires dipping into mercury were amalgamated with mercurous nitrate, which made the connections very perfect.

In measuring the resistances of the armature and of the armature and leaders, the 'Wheatstone's bridge was used, and Thomson's reflecting galvanometer in place of the small galvanometer usually employed. The resistance of the armature mains and leaders was between .17 and .18 Ohm. When the bridge indicated .17

the galvanometer showed a deflection of 29.5 divisions ; when it indicated .18 the galvanometer showed an opposite deflection of 45. From this we get the resistance of the armature mains and leaders, .17395 Ohm.

The main alone measured .14460, leaving for the resistance of the armature and leaders to the binding parts .029 Ohm.

Leading wires being clamped on the commutator the resistance measured in several positions was .16207. These leaders measured .14604, leaving for the resistance of the armature alone .016 Ohm.

The resistance of the field magnet coils was 37. Ohms.

TEST BY VOLTAMETER.

Before making the test the generator was run for some time to allow the circuit to heat up, and the resistance of the line measured from time to time until it was found to remain constant. The voltameter was then introduced into the circuit and allowed to remain fifteen minutes.

During this time the speed of the dynamometer was determined for ten minutes,
and the average speed computed.

The deflection of the pendulum was observed every three minutes and the average taken, although the variation was only
one degree. At the end of the test the circuit
was broken and the resistance again
measured, and it was found not to have
changed perceptibly.

The plates were then removed, washed
in water, then in alcohol. and dried in a
gentle heat. They were then weighed
carefully.

DATA OBTAINED FROM THE TEST.

Weight of copper gained by negative
plates = 24.465 m. g.
Time of test = 15 minutes.
Weight gained per second = 27.183 m. g.
Average speed of dynamometer = 400.5
rev. per min.
Average deflection of pendulum = 42° 20'.
Resistance of iron wire = .76 Ohm.
Resistance of iron wires and magnet coils
in multiple arc = .744 Ohm.

Total resistance of circuit $= .744 + .029 =$ .773 Ohm.

Internal resistance of armature $= .016$ Ohm.

RESULTS OBTAINED FROM DATA.

Value of current in webers $= \dfrac{27.183}{.32456} =$ 83.753.

Electrical energy $(83.753)^2 \times .773 \times 44.24 =$ 239880.726 ft. lbs. per minute.

Energy indicated by dynamometer 171.2 $\times (\sin 42° = .67344) \times 4505 \times 6.2832$ $= 290125.54$ ft. lbs. per minute.

Friction of dynamometer and generator 290125.54 $\times .135 = 39166.9479$ ft. lbs. per minute.

Energy used in turning armature in field of force $290125.54 \times 855 = 250958.59$ ft. lbs. per minute.

Friction of dynamometer alone $= 290125.5$ $\times .109 = 31623.68$ ft. lbs. per minute.

Energy actually applied to armature pulley $290125.54 \times .891 = 258501.96$ ft lbs. per min.

Of the total electrical energy 239880.7

$$\frac{.016}{.773} = 4965.189 \text{ appeared in the armature,}$$

$$\frac{.744}{.773 \times 49.68} \times 239880.726 = 4647.39 \text{ in the}$$

magnet coils, and 230268.176 ft. lbs. per minute in the external circuit.

The efficiency of the generator is the ratio of the energy required to turn the armature in the magnetic field, to the total electrical energy developed $= \frac{239880.726}{250958.59} = .955.$

The commercial efficiency is the ratio of the energy required to drive the machine (including friction) to the electrical energy which appears in the external circuit $= \frac{230268.169}{258501.96} = .8608.$

TEST BY MEANS OF THE CALORIMETER.

As in the voltametric test the generator was first run until the circuit was thoroughly heated, and the same care was taken to determine the speed and deflection of the dynamometer. When the calorimeter was thrown into the circuit an

approximately equal resistance was thrown
out so as not to change the total resistance too much. At the end of the test
the resistance of the circuit was measured
carefully as soon as the circuit was broken
and before the wires became cooled.

DATA OBTAINED FROM THIS TEST.

Water in calorimeter = 77 lbs.

Connection for waste heat = 1.78 lbs.

Range of temperature = $79° - 69.8° =$
9.2°F.

Specific heat for this range = 1.0015.

Average speed of dynamometer =394 rev.
per min.

Average deflection of pendulum = 43° 24′
(sin =.68709).

Time of tests = 16 minutes.

Resistance of iron wires and calorimeter
coil = .68 Ohm.

This and magnet coil in multiple arc =
.667 Ohm.

Total resistance of circuit .667 + .029 =
.696.

Resistance of calorimeter coil = .1 Ohm.

RESULTS OBTAINED FROM THESE DATA.

Energy developed in calorimeter =
$$\frac{78118 \times 1.0015 \times 9.2 \times 772}{16} = 35022.897 \text{ ft.lbs.}$$
per minute.

Total electrical energy
35022.897 × 6.96 = 243759.36 ft. lbs. per minute.

Energy indicated by dynamometer =
171.2 × .68709 × 894 × 6.2832
= 291201.46 ft. lbs. per min.

Energy used in turning armature in field of force
291201.46 × .865 =
251889.265 ft. lbs. per min.

Energy actually applied to armature pulley
291201.46 × .891 =
259460.5 ft. lbs. per min.

Of the electrical energy
$$243759.36 \times \frac{.016}{.696} = 5603.66$$
appeared in the armature
$$243759.36 \times \frac{.667}{.669 \times 54.41} = 4215.89$$

in the magnet coils; and 233939.81 ft. lbs.
per minute appeared outside.

$$\text{Efficiency} = \frac{243759363}{251889.265} = 967.$$

$$\text{Commercial efficiency} = \frac{233939.81}{259460.5} = .901.$$

TEST BY MEASUREMENT OF THE ELECTRO-MOTIVE FORCE AND RESISTANCE.

In this test the electro-motive force was measured between the binding posts of the generator, and the external resistance was measured between the same points.

The deflection and speed of the dynamometer were measured at the same time, the electro-motive force was observed and the resistance was measured just before and after these observations and was the same in both cases.

DATA OBTAINED FROM THIS TEST.

Electro-motive force = 53 volts.
Resistance of circuit (external) .64 Ohm.
Resistance between binding posts .629.
Average speed of dynamometer, 355 rev.
    per min.

Average deflection, 42° (nat.sine=.66913).
Total resistance of circuit, .658.

RESULTS OBTAINED FROM THESE DATA.

Energy developed in external circuit

$$\frac{(53^2)}{629} \times 44.24 = 197567.43 \text{ ft. lbs. per min.}$$

Total electrical energy

$$197567.43 \times \frac{.658}{.629} = 206673.0295 \text{ ft. lbs. per min.}$$

Energy in armature

$$206673.029 \times \frac{.016}{.658} = 5025.5.$$

Energy in magnet coils

$$\frac{(53^2)}{37} \times 44.24 = 3346.667 \text{ ft. lbs. per min.}$$

Energy in external circuit 198300.88 ft. lbs. per min.

Energy indicated by dynamometer
$171.2 \times .66913 \times 355 \times 62332 =$
$2553 + 9.04$ ft. lbs. per min.

Energy used in turning armature in field of force
$255519.04 \times .865 =$
221023.97 ft. lbs. per min.

Energy actually applied to armature pulley

$$255519.04 \times .891 =$$

$$227667.47 \text{ ft. lbs. per min.}$$

$$\text{Efficiency} = \frac{206673.0295}{221023.97} = .935.$$

$$\text{Commercial efficiency} = \frac{198300.88}{227667.47} = .87.$$

Average efficiency, .951.

Average commercial efficiency, .887.

ECONOMY OF THE CONDUCTORS.

The economy of the conductors which convey the electricity from the generator to the lamps may be considered under two heads: first, the efficiency of the material, second, the efficiency of its dimensions.

The efficiency of any material is determined by its price and conductivity as compared with other materials. The two materials most commonly used for conductors are copper and iron. The present price of copper is about seven times the price of iron and its conductivity is about six times as great; thus the actual cost of a line of copper wire of a given conductivity is one-sixth greater than iron wire of the same conductivity. Copper wire,

however, is much more uniform than iron
wire: it is free from cinder streaks that
are so common to iron wire. and is much
more pliable and less bulky. and therefore
less difficult to handle. For electric-light
mains. which have to be frequently tapped,
copper wire seems to be preferable to iron
wire.

2D. THE EFFICIENCY OF DIMENSIONS.

This is determined by the cost of the
conductor and the loss of energy in the
conductor. As the energy developed in
different parts of the circuit varies directly
as the resistance of these parts, some
energy must appear in the conductors.
This energy appears as heat, and is lost.

The most efficient dimensions of the
conductors depend upon the amount of
energy to be transmitted and the distance
which it is to be transmitted.

To secure maximum efficiency, therefore, we would have to calculate the most
efficient size under all conditions as to
number of lamps and distances. Know-
ing. however, the conditions most usually

met in practice, we can determine that loss of energy in the conductors, which is usually most efficient, and expressing this loss as a percentage of the total energy transmitted, calculate the size of our conductors upon this basis by making the resistance of the conductors the same percentage of the total resistance of the circuit, as the loss of energy allowed is of the total energy transmitted.

Thus, when we wish to calculate the dimensions of our conductors necessary to convey the current to a given number of lamps a given distance, allowing a loss of $\frac{1}{n}$ of the total energy, we must determine the resistance of our lamps and make the resistance of our conductors $\frac{1}{n-1}$ part of the resistance of the lamps.

Thus we see that the cost of the conductors necessary to carry the current for a given number of lamps a given distance varies inversely as the resistance of the lamps, and although we can make a high or a low resistance lamp of the same economy, it will cost less to convey the current to a given number of high-resistance lamps a given distance, than it will to convey the current to the same number of low resistance lamps the same distance.

ECONOMY OF THE LAMPS.

The economy of the lamps is determined by the energy consumed and the amount of light produced; in determining the energy consumed in the lamps, the electro-motive force was measured between the terminals of the lamps, and also the resistance, and the energy determined in foot pounds per minute by the formula $\dfrac{e^2}{R}$ 44.24.

In measuring the electro-motive force the same arrangements were used as in determining the electro-motive force of the generator, but the damping magnet was adjusted to give three units of deflection to a volt instead of five. To measure the resistance of the lamps when burning, the current was divided into two parts, one part was passed through the lamp and the other through a variable resistance, when

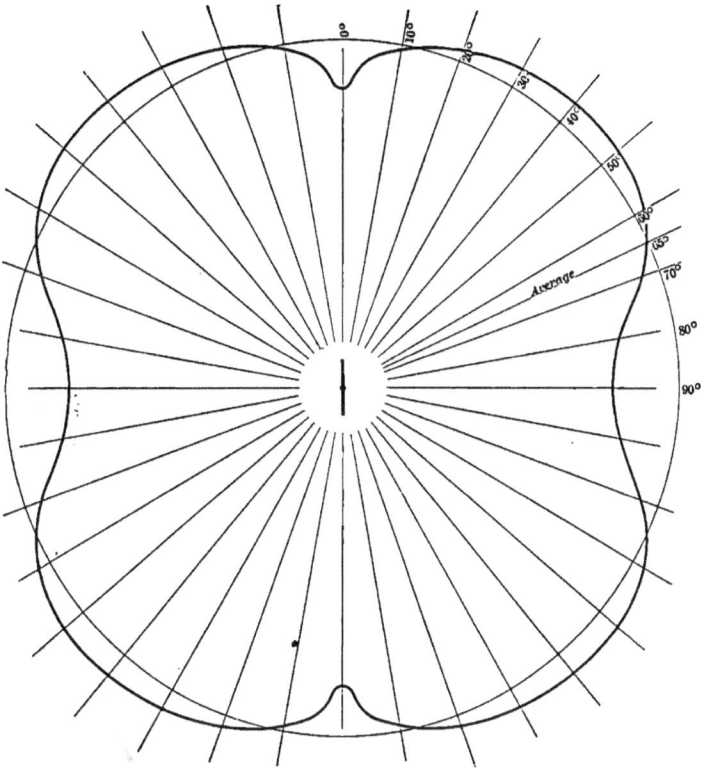

CURVE SHOWING ILLUMINATION OF EDISON'S LAMP IN A HORIZONTAL PLANE.

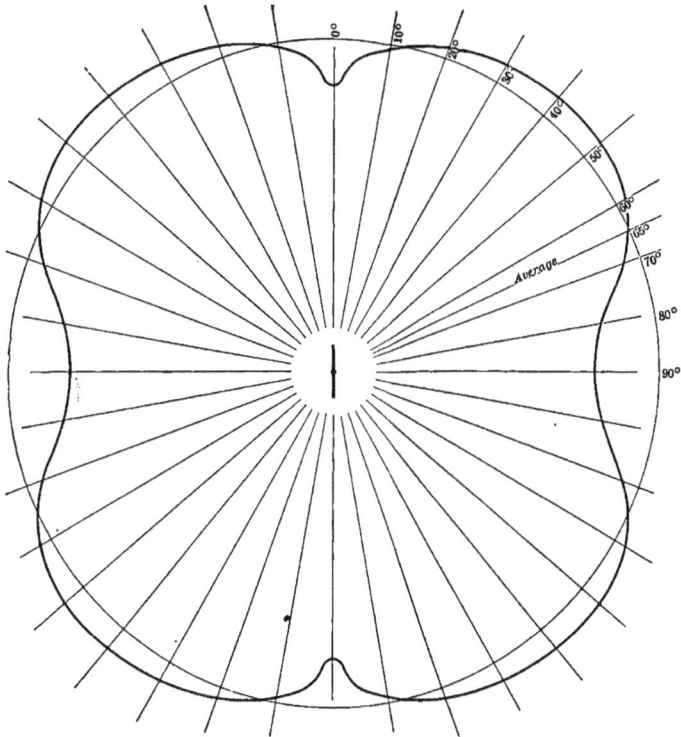

CURVE SHOWING ILLUMINATION OF EDISON'S LAMP IN A HORIZONTAL PLANE.

~

both were passed through a differential galvanometer, but in opposite directions; when the current was the same in both branches, the needle of the galvanometer would indicate zero. As the electro-motive forces of the two branches were equal, their currents were equal, when their resistances were equal, so by altering the variable resistance until the needle came to zero, and measuring the variable resistance we thus determined the resistance of the lamp while it was burning. This variable resistance was measured each time before it cooled.

As the light given out in a horizontal plane varies at different angles, the angle of average illumination was first determined for the lamp used, which was the Edison lamp. To determine this angle, the candle pov r was measured every 10° through a quar t, and the candle power observed laid oi on a suitable scale on lines radiated from a point. A curve was drawn through the points thus determined, and the four quadrants being made symmetrical, its area was determined and a circle of equal area drawn about the point from which the lines radiate. The points where this circle cut the curve determine the angle at which the candle power is the same that it would be if the light were evenly distributed.

Having determined the angular position of these points with reference to the plane of the carbon, all measurements were made with the axis of the photometer in this angle.

To insure that the lamp was in this position, it was twisted until the shadow of the carbon fell on the center of the disc and then turned through an angle of 65°, which the curve shows to be the proper angle. All measurements of lamps were made at the angle of equal illumination.

In order to determine the economy of a lamp at different degrees of incandescence, an Edison lamp was measured at intensities ranging from a dull red to 40 candle power, and the results plotted in a curve show a rapid rise in economy as the candle power increases. While the economy of a lamp increases with incandescence, its life shortens, but as I have had neither

10   15   20   25   30   35   40   45   Candle Power

NCE.

time nor opportunities for life tests, I cannot give data for life at various degrees of incandescence.

Mr. Edison's standard of illumination has been 16 candle power, and his aim has been to produce a lamp that will give good economy and a reasonable life at that candle power.

To determine the energy consumed by these lamps when burning at their normal candle power, five lamps, as made at present by Mr. Edison, were tested with the following results :

TABLE SHOWING ENERGY CONSUMED BY EDISON
LAMPS.

	Candle Power.	Volts.	Ohms.	Foot-pounds of Electricity per minute.
1	16	98.66	135.5	3178 −03
2	16	98.66	142.5	3021−91
3	16	99.	140.5	3107−41
4	16	98.	148.5	2861−15
5	16	99.33	131.5	3319−32

Showing an average of 3,097−564 ft.

CURVE SHOWING RELATION BETWEEN ECONOMY AND INCANDESCENCE.

lbs. of electricity per minute, or 10.65 lamps per h. p. of electricity, giving 170 candles per h. p.

Mr. Edison gets 10.65 lamps per horse power of electricity, but as he allows a loss of 10% of the electrical energy used in the lamps upon the conductors, he gets 9.68 lamps for each h. p. of electricity generaated. As the average commercial efficiency of this generator is .887, this gives him 8.58 lamps per dynamometrical h. p.

The report of the Board of Commissioners of the Millers' Exhibition, held in Cincinnati just one year ago, gives the results of the trial of three modern steam engines.

These results show an average for the three engines of .878 of the indicated power converted into useful work; using this factor for the conversion of dynamometrical into indicated horse power, we find that Mr. Edison gets 7.62 lamps per indicated horse power.

ON THE

DYNAMO-ELECTRIC CURRENT,

AND ON

CERTAIN MEANS TO IMPROVE ITS STEADINESS.

By C. WILLIAM SIEMENS, D.C.L., F.R.S.

From Philosophical Transactions of the Royal Society.

Steadiness of the Electric Current.

On the 14th of February, 1867, I communicated a short paper to the Royal Society, describing the accumulative or dynamo-electrical principle of action, the conception of which I attributed to my brother Dr. Werner Siemens. When the paper was read, another paper followed by Sir Charles Wheatstone (sent in on the 24th February) also describing this principle of action, thus showing that the same line of thought had occupied that eminent philosopher.

In illustration of my paper I exhibited a machine of my design, embodying the accumulative principle of action, which furnished abundant evidence of the powerful nature of the current that could be thus produced. It consisted of two horseshoe electro magnets, between the poles of which a Siemens armature could be made to rotate, the machine being furnished with a handle or pulley for that purpose. A commutator was provided, by which the alternating currents set up in the rotating coil (after a first impulse had been given) were directed through the coils of the stationary electro magnets in a continuous manner, and proceeded thence outward to ignite a platinum wire of some 12″ in length, or to perform other work.

This machine, although the first of its kind, has done good service ever since its construction, having been found very efficacious in exciting powerful permanent magnets at the telegraph works of Siemens Brothers at Woolwich.

Since 1867 the accumulative principle has been employed in the machines of different makers, and one form of dynamo-electric machine, that of M. Gramme, differs very materially from the machine above referred to, and had met very deservedly with extensive recognition. M. Gramme embodied in his machine the principle of Professor Pacinotti's magnetic ring, which enabled him to produce powerful electric currents without much of the loss of energy caused in previous machines through the heating of the rotating armature.

Another modification of the dynamo-electrical machine is one devised by Mr. Von Heftner Alteneck, an engineer and physicist employed under my brother Werner Siemens, at Berlin. This machine differs from that first submitted by myself in several important particulars. Instead of the Werner Siemens armature, Von Heftner Alteneck adopted a rotating coil of iron wire wound with insulated copper wire in more than one direction, the several coils of wire being connected seriatim with the commutator, and through it, with the wire surrounding the soft iron bars, and with the electric lamp or other resistance on the outer circuit.

The advantage claimed for this mode of construction is that all the wire forming the rotating coil or helix is brought into the magnetic field, excepting only those portions crossing from side to side of the coil; and in order to reduce this unproductive resistance to a minimum, the rotating coil or helix has been made comparatively long, and the number of electro magnets has been increased generally to six or more.

The principal advantage of the dynamoelectrical machine over all other current generators consists in its power of producing currents of great magnitude, and of an intensity up to 100 volts, with a small primary resistance, and therefore with a comparatively small expenditure of mechanical energy. It labors, on the other hand, under the disadvantage that the power of the current depends, at a given velocity, upon the magnetic force developed in the electro magnets. This force depends upon the amount of current passing through the coils of the magnets, which in its turn is dependent in an inverse ratio upon the resistance in the outer circuit. If from some accidental cause the external resistance is increased, the electro-motive force of the machine, instead of rising to overcome the obstruction, diminishes, and thus aggravates the resulting disturbance. If, on the other hand, the resistance of the outer circuit diminishes, as in the case when the carbons of an electric regulator touch one another, the electro magnets are immediately excited to a maximum, and the electro-motive force of the machine is increased. The power absorbed and its equivalent, the heat generated in the circuit, is equal to the square of the electro-motive force divided by the resistance; hence the work demanded from the engine will be greatly increased, the machine may be dangerously overheated, and powerful sparks may injure the commutator. It is chiefly owing to this instability of the dynamo-electric current that its application to electric illumination has been retarded, and that magneto-electric machines and machines producing alternating currents have been again used, although they are inferior to the dynamo machine in the current energy produced for a given expenditure of mechanical energy.

The properties of dynamo-electric machines have been examined by several observers. Messrs. Houston and Thomson (Franklin Institute) compared the efficiency of the Gramme, Brush, and Wallace Farmer machines. Dr. Hopkinson (Institution of Mechanical Engineers, 25th April, 1879) examined a medium-sized Siemens machine, determined its efficiency, and expressed the electromotive force as a function of the current. Herrn Mayer and Anerbach (*Wiedemanns' Annalen*, November, 1879) and M. Mascart have experimented on the Gramme machine, and Mr. Schwendler on both Gramme and Siemens machines.

The radical defect of the dynamo machine of ordinary construction, may be inferred from the results of these experiments. The remedy has, however, been in our hands from the time of the first announcement of the principle of these machines before the Royal Society, when Sir Charles Wheatstone pointed out that "a very remarkable increase of all the effects, accompanied by a diminution in the resistance of the machine, is observed when a cross wire is placed so as to divert a great portion of the current from the electro magnet."

Some of the constructors of dynamo machines, namely: Mr. Ladd in this country, and Mr. Brush in the United States of America, have taken advantage of this suggestion, the latter with the avowed object in view of obviating spontaneous changes of polarity in effecting electro precipitation of metals, and without perhaps having realized all of the advantages of which this mode of action is capable; others have refrained from doing so on account of difficulties resulting, as I shall endeavor to show, from an insufficient examination into some important physical conditions that require attention in order to realize economical results.

An ordinary medium-sized Siemens-Alteneck dynamo-electrical machine has wound on its rotating helix insulated copper wire of 2.5 m.m. diameter in 24 sections, representing a resistance of .4014

S. U.* The four electro-magnet coils connected seriatim are composed of copper wire of 5.5 m.m. diameter, presenting a total resistance of 0.3065 S. U.

If (as has frequently been done) the wires of this machine were to be connected as suggested in Sir Charles Wheatstone's original paper, thus making the outer circuit not continuous with but parallel to the coil circuit, and if the outer circuit had a resistance of one unit, it would follow that the total resistance to the current set up by the rotation of the armature would be reduced from

$$.4 + .3 + 1. = 1.7 \text{ to } .4 + \frac{.3 \times 1}{1 + .3} = 0.61 \text{ unit,}$$

* The resistance coils used in these experiments were graduated according to the mercury system introduced by Dr. Werner Siemens, and adopted by the Telegraphic Convention at Vienna in 1868. The B. A. unit was determined in 1874 by Kohlrausch to be 1.0493 S. U., or combined with Lorenz's value of the S. U. afterwards adopted, 0.9797×10⁹ C.G. S. units—as much as 2 per cent. below its ascribed theoretical value. Later determinations by H. F. Weber (Phil. Mag., March, 1878) makes the S. U. to be equal to 0.955×10⁹ C. G. S. units, and thus the Ohm to be 0.2 per cent. higher than its ascribed value; if this latter value is used, the numerical results must be correspondingly altered.

causing a great increase of current, the major portion (in the proportion of 10 to 4) would flow through the electro magnets, thus causing a great increase of heating effect. The resistance of the field magnet must therefore be greatly increased, but if it were attempted to increase that resistance simply by reducing the diameter of the wire, and increasing the number of convolutions until the same thickness of coil was obtained, the magnetic excitement and with it the electro-motive force of the current produced at a given velocity of rotation would suffer a material decrease. The current flowing through the helix coil would moreover have to divide itself, and in order to reach the same limit in the outer circuit its intensity in the helix coil would have to be increased, causing it to heat more readily than before. It was necessary, therefore, to raise the effect of the magnet current to the same level as before with as small a proportion of the helix current as possible, in order to leave a maximum proportion of the current for the outer circuit. In order to effect this, the magnet bars had to be increased in length, and placed further apart so as to provide room for coils of greatly increased weight and dimensions; at the same time the helix wire had to be increased in diameter to give room for the aggregate current, but in reality I found it advantageous to increase the diameter of the same in a much greater proportion.

These general conditions having been determined by preliminary experiment, Mr. Lauckert, electrician engaged at my works, undertook a series of comparative experiments which are given in the appendix attached to this paper, and the results are given numerically and exhibited in curves. On examining the curves it will be remarked:

1. That the electro-motive force instead of diminishing with increased resistance, increases at first rapidly, then more slowly towards an asymptote.

2. That the current in the outer circuit is actually greater for a unit and a·half resistance than for one unit.

3. With an external resistance of one unit, which is about equivalent to an electric arc when 30 or 40 webers are passing through it, 2.44 horse power is expended, of which 1.29 horse power is usefully employed; an efficiency of 53 per cent. as compared with 45 per cent. in the case of the ordinary dynamo machine.

4. That the maximum energy which can be demanded from the engine is 2.6 horse power, so that but a small margin of power is needed to suffice for the greatest possible requirement.

5. That the maximum energy which can be injuriously transferred into heat in the machine itself is 1.3 horse power, so that there is no fear here of destroying the insulation of the helix by excessive heating.

6. That the maximum current is approximately that which would be habitually used, and which the commutator and collecting brushes are quite capable of transmitting.

Hence I conclude that the new machine will give a steadier light than the old one, with greater average economy of power, that it will be less liable to derangement, and may be driven without variation of speed by a smaller engine; also that the new machine is free from the objection of having its currents reversed when used for the purpose of electro deposition.

The same peculiarity also enables me to effect an important simplification of the regulator to work electric lamps, to dispense with all wheel and clock-work in the arrangement, as shown in Fig. 1. The two carbons, being pushed onward by gravity or spring power, are checked laterally by a pointed metallic abutment, situated at such a distance from the arc itself that the heat is only just sufficient to cause the gradual wasting away of the carbon in contact with atmospheric air. The carbon holders are connected with the iron core of a solenoid coil, of a resistance equal to about fifty times that of the arc, the ends of which coil are connected with the two electrodes respectively. The weight of the core, which has

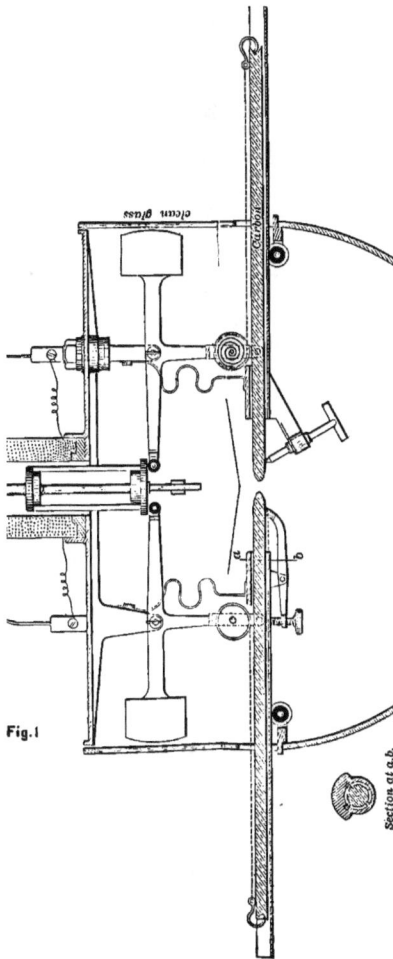

Fig. 1

electric glass

Carbon

Section at a.b.

v
t
a
s
ɪ
ł
f

t
,¹
·I
t
t
ε
l
ε
i
t
(
r
·ł
ε
t
ɪ
i

to be maintained in suspension by the attractive force produced by the current, determines the distance between the electrodes, and hence the electric resistance of the arc. The result is that the length of the arc is regulated automatically so as to maintain a uniform resistance, signifying a uniform development of light.

APPENDIX.

The measurements of the electric currents were made with an electro dynamometer, the movable part of which consisted of a single turn of 4 m.m. wire, and the stationary coil of nine turns of the same.

To be able to reduce the electrical measurements into absolute power developed, it was in the first place necessary to determine the constant of the instrument in use. This was done in the following manner: Five copper plates of about $11'' \times 8''$ were connected as shown in the sketch.

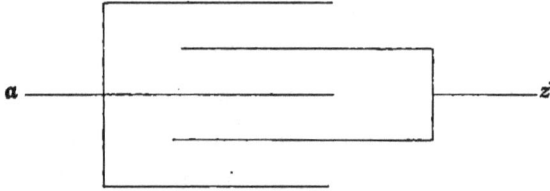

These were carefully weighed and immersed in a solution of sulphate of copper. The machine was previously started, the time of immersion carefully noted, and the readings of the current taken every half minute. The plates were so arranged that the current entering at a and leaving at z deposited the copper on both sides of the plate at z. After a certain time the plates were taken out, quickly rinsed in water, and dried in sawdust. The plates were then carefully weighed again and the deposit calculated per degree reading on the instrument per second of time. Six independent measurements were taken with currents varying from 20 to 40 webers, and gave a mean of .000779 gramme of copper per second per degree reading. The differences of these measurements from the mean varied from 0.21

per cent. to 6.6 per cent., the mean of the differences being 1.98 per cent.

According to F. Kohlrausch (Pogg. Ann., Bd. cxlix., 1873) the quantity of silver deposited by the C. G. S. unit of electricity is 0.011363 gramme, and since the quantities vary as the equivalents of the metals deposited, we have

$$\frac{.011363 \times 63.5}{216} = 0.003340$$

gramme of copper.

One weber being $\frac{1}{10}$ C. G. S. unit, we have to divide by 10 the quantity of copper deposited by a current of one weber in one second, that is .000334 gramme, and dividing .000779 by .000334 we get 2.23323 webers for a degree reading of our instrument.

To be able to compare the machines having the new winding (*i. e.*, the wire on the electro magnets connected parallel with the outer circuit) with the ordinary machines, it was necessary to experiment on the relation existing between the power expended and the current produced with different resistances in circuit and different speeds.

. A medium dynamo machine with 24 part commutator was used, the helix being wound with 336 convolutions of 2.5 m. m. wire, having a resistance of .4014 S. U. when measured in the machine. The electro magnets were wound with four layers of 5.5 m.m. wire, each having 32 convolutions, and therefore the four bobbins a total of 512 convolutions with a resistance of .3065 S. U.

The accompanying Tables Nos. 5, 6, 7, 8, and 9 give the details of the experiments made, which are shown graphically in the diagrams similarily numbered. The current in webers was simply calculated by multiplying the square root of the reading on the electro dynamometer with the constant of the instrument, i. e., 2.3323.

To be able to calculate the electromotive force from the current in webers and resistance in Siemens' units, it was necessary to convert the S. U. into C.G.S. units by multiplying the same by .9337 ×

10^9. (This figure is given by Lorenz, Pogg. Ann., Bd. cxlix., 1873.) By again multiplying this resistance into the current we get, according to Ohm's law, the electro-motive force in C. G. S. units, and by dividing by 10^8 we get the E. M. F. in volts.

I have further calculated the total amount of work developed in the following manner:

Work done $=E \times C \times t$, or, which is the same, $C^2 \times R \times t$, where E is E. M. F; C, current; R, resistance; t, time.

From these calculations t is eliminated as it occurs in all the equations.

1 volt $=10^8$ C. G. S. units.

1 weber $=\frac{1}{10}$ C. G. S. unit of current.

1 HP $=7.46 \times 10^9$ C. G. S. units.

Therefore

$$\frac{1 \text{ volt} \times 1 \text{ weber}}{1 \text{ HP}} = \frac{10^8 \times 10^{-1}}{7.46 \times 10^9} = \frac{1}{746}$$

and if we multiply the E. M. F. in volts by the current in webers, and divide by 746, we have the actual work developed in horse power.

To find the actual work done in the outside resistance we use the formula $C^2 \times R$, of course having to reduce the resistance R into absolute C. G. S. units by multiplying by .9337 × 10 .

The machine with the new winding had a helix with 24 part commutator wound with 312 convolutions of 2.8 m.m. wire.

The electro-magnets being lengthened by 2″ to take bobbins $10\frac{1}{2}″$, instead of $8\frac{1}{2}″$ as on the ordinary machines, I had three sets of bobbins made, and had the same wound with different sizes of wire, viz.; 2.5 m.m., 2.8 m.m., and 3 m.m., having a respective resistance of 11.26, 7.563, and 4.46 S. U.

The accompanying Tables Nos. 1, 2, 3, and 4 show the experiments made with this machine with electro-magnets of 11.26 S. U. resistance; Nos. 10, 11, 12, and 13 with electro-magnets of 7.563 S.U.; and Nos. 14 and 15 with electro-magnets of 4.46 S. U. The helix in all cases having been wound with 2.8 m.m. wire with a resistance of .234 S. U. when measured in the machine.

The Tables marked 5, 6, 7, 8, and 9 refer to the dynamo machine wound in the ordinary way.

The Tables marked 16, 17, 18, 19, 20, 21, 22, and 23 show the results obtained with a machine having a helix wound with 288 convolutions of 3 m.m. wire and a resistance of .173 S. units. The electromagnets, as before, had a resistance of 11.26, 7.563, and 4.47 S. U.

No. 1.

Helix: 24 part commutator, 312 convolutions, 2.8 m.m. wire, .234 S. U. resistance.
Electro-magnets: 3916 convolutions, 2.5 m.m. wire, 11.26 S. U. resistance (connected parallel to outer circuit).

Revolutions per minute.	Resistance in S. U.		Reading on electro-dynamometer.			Current in webers.			E. M. F. in helix in volts.	Horse power.			Percentage of energy turned into useful work.
	In outer circuit.	Total in circuit.	Helix.	Electro-magnet.	Outer circuit.	Helix.	Electro-magnet.	Outer circuit.		Expended	Developed Total.	Developed in outer circuit.	
500	0.0	.25	0.0			1.63			.3804	.205	.000831		
"	.01	.26	.5			1.63			.3957	"	.000864		
"	.02	.28	.5			2.33			.6091	"	.00190		
"	.05	.34	1.0			2.86			.9079	"	.00348		
"	.10	.48	1.5			3.30			1.479	"	.00654		
"	.25	.72	2.0			8.80			5.915	"	.0698	.0409	5.73
"	.50	.94	14.0	1.0	12	26.58	2.33	8.08	23.32	.714	.881	.587	41.04
"	.75	1.16	180.0	1.5	115	31.30	2.86	25.01	33.90	1.43	1.422	.987	53.93
"	1.0	1.36	180.0	2.0	145	28.08	3.30	28.08	35.65	1.83	1.342	1.063	58.08
"	1.25	1.56	145.0	2.0	125	27.09	3.30	26.07	39.46	"	1.433	1.17	63.93
"	1.5	1.75	135.0	3.0	115	26.79	4.04	25.01	43.77	"	1.592	1.21	66.12
"	1.75	1.94	132.0	3.0	102	25.55	4.04	23.55	46.28	1.73	1.585	1.29	69.94
"	2.0		120.0	3.5	95		4.36	22.73		.714			
"	∞		5.0	4.0	0	5.21	4.66						

No. 2.

Helix: 24 part commutator, 312 convolutions, 2.8 m.m. wire, .234 S. U. resistance.
Electro-magnets: 3916 convolutions, 2.5 m.m. wire, 11.26 S. U. resistance (connected parallel to outer circuit).

Revolutions per minute.	Resistance in S. U.		Reading on electro-dynamometer.			Current in webers.			E. M. F. in helix in volts.	Horse power.			Percentage of energy turned into useful work.
	In outer circuit.	Total in circuit.	Helix.	Electro-magnet.	Outer circuit.	Helix.	Electro-magnet.	Outer circuit.		Expended.	Total developed.	Developed in outer circuit.	
600	0.0	.24	0	...	...	...	...	...	1.044	.245	.0032	...	...
"	.25	.48	1	...	...	2.23	...	...	3.502	"	.0244	...	...
"	.50	.72	5	...	115	5.21	...	25.01	22.87	"	.799	.587	34.24
"	.75	.94	125	2.0	175	26.07	3.3	30.86	37.04	1.714	1.70	1.16	47.34
"	1.0	1.16	215	2.5	153	34.20	3.69	28.84	41.35	2.45	1.805	1.3	53.06
"	1.25	1.36	195	3.5	144	32.57	4.361	27.99	46.20	"	1.96	1.47	63.09
"	1.50	1.56	185	4.0	125	31.72	4.66	26.07	48.80	2.33	1.95	1.49	67.72
"	1.75	1.75	164	4.0	120	29.87	4.66	25.55	53.43	2.20	2.12	1.633	74.22
"	2.0	1.94	160	5.0		29.50			65.66	"			
"	8	11.50	6		0	5.71	5.21	...		1.10	.508	...	...

No. 3.

Helix: 24 part commutator, 312 convolutions, 2.8 m.m. wire, .234 S. U. resistance. Electro-magnets: 3916 convolutions, 2.5 m.m. wire, 11.26 S. U. resistance (connected parallel to outer circuit).

Revolutions per minute.	Resistance in S. U.		Reading on electro-dynamometer.			Current in webers.			E. M. F. in helix in volts.	Horse power.			Percentage of energy turned into useful work.
	In outer circuit.	Total in circuit.	Helix.	Electro-magnet.	Outer circuit.	Helix.	Electro-magnet.	Outer circuit.		Expended.	Total developed.	Developed in outer circuit. *f*	
700	0.0	.24	:	:	:	4.66	:	:	2.078	.20	.0129	:	:
:	.25	.48	4	:	:	7.74	:	:	5.203	:	.0540	:	:
:	.5	.72	11	5	255	39.37	5.21	37.25	34.56	:	1.82	1.3	55.58
:	.75	.94	285	6	280	42.05	5.71	39.03	46.33	2.57	2.61	1.0	54.75
:	1.0	1.18	325	6	250	40.40	5.71	36.88	51.3	3.47	2.77	2.13	61.37
:	1.25	1.36	300	6	205	38.75	5.71	33.39	55.81	:	2.90	2.09	60.23
:	1.5	1.56	276	6	170	35.37	5.71	30.41	57.79	:	2.74	2.03	58.50
:	1.75	1.75	230	7	158	34.2	6.17	29.31	61.95	3.28	2.84	2.15	65.54
:	2.0	1.94	215	10	0	7.74	7.37	:	88.11	1.29	.862	:	:
:	8	11.50	11	:	:	:	:	:	:	:	:	:	:

No. 4.

Helix: 24 part commutator, 312 convolutions, 2.8 m.m. wire, .234 S. U. resistance. Electro-magnets: 3916 convolutions, 2.5 m.m. wire, 11.26 S. U. resistance (connected parallel to outer circuit).

Revolutions per minute.	Resistance in S. U.		Reading on electro-dynamometer.			Current in webers.			E. M. F. in helix in volts.	Horse power.			Percentage of energy turned into useful work.
	In outer circuit.	Total in circuit.	Helix.	Electro-magnet.	Outer circuit.	Helix.	Electro-magnet.	Outer circuit.		Expended.	Total developed.	Developed in outer circuit.	
758	12.30	6.11	38	9.0	9	14.38	6.99	6.99	82.03	2.78	1.58	.752	27.26
756	8.90	5.21	49	8.5	14	16.32	6.77	8.88	79.38	2.93	1.74	.872	29.96
734	6.00	4.15	69	9.0	28	19.37	6.99	12.34	75.05	3.0	1.95	1.14	38.00
758	6.00	4.15	72	9.0	28	19.79	6.99	12.34	76.67	3.09	2.03	1.14	36.89
750	4.50	3.43	85	9.0	34	21.50	6.17	13.61	68.85	3.21	1.98	1.04	32.40
756	3.50	2.91	150	7.0	87	28.56	5.71	21.75	77.59	3.86	2.97	2.17	52.07
760	3.00	2.61	185	6.0	107	31.72	5.21	24.12	77.30	3.88	3.29	2.18	56.18
758	2.50	2.28	204	5.0	130	33.31	..	26.58	70.91	3.87	3.17	2.21	57.11
750	2.25	2.12	230	..	150	35.37	..	28.56	70.01	3.83	3.32	2.30	60.01
760	2.00	1.94	226	..	157	35.06	..	29.27	63.51	3.88	2.99	2.14	55.15

No. 4.—Continued.

Revolutions per minute.	Resistance in S. U. Outer circuit.	Resistance in S. U. Total in circuit.	Reading on electro-dynamometer. Helix.	Reading on electro-dynamometer. Electro-magnet.	Reading on electro-dynamometer. Outer circuit.	Current in webers. Helix.	Current in webers. Electro-magnet.	Current in webers. Outer circuit.	E. M. F. in helix in volts.	Horse power. Expended.	Horse power. Total developed.	Horse power. Developed in outer circuit.	Percentage of energy turned into useful work.
755	1.75	1.75	252		180	37.03		31.30	60.50	3.85	3.00	2.14	55.58
754	1.50	1.56	255		185	37.25		31.72	54.26	3.85	2.71	1.89	49.10
760	1.35	1.44	305		240	41.30		36.14	54.71	3.72	2.99	2.21	59.41
756	1.25	1.36	310		245	41.06		36.50	52.14	3.70	2.89	2.08	56.48
764	1.10	1.24	315		260	41.20		37.61	47.70	3.74	2.63	1.94	51.87
766	1.00	1.16	315		264	40.73		37.89	44.62	3.59	2.46	1.80	50.01
750	.90	1.07	285		238	39.37		35.98	39.33	3.06	2.07	1.46	47.71
765	.80	.99	235		205	35.75		33.39	33.04	2.50	1.58	1.12	44.80
760	.75	.94	208		185	33.64		31.30	29.52	2.48	1.33	.92	37.09
755	.65	.85	98		87	23.09		21.75	18.32	1.08	.567	.385	35.64
760	.60	.81	50		45	16.49		15.64	12.47	1.08	.275	.184	17.03
700	.55	.76	30		25	12.77		11.68	9.07	.43	.155	.094	21.86
752	.50	.72	12		10	8.07		7.37	6.36	.46	.069	.034	7.39
..	.40	.65	5		4	5.21		4.66	3.16	..	.0221	.0109	2.37
..	8	11.50	12	12.00	..	8.07	8.07	..	86.64	..	.937	..	..

No. 5.

Helix: 24 part commutator, 336 convolutions, 2.5 m.m. wire,, 4014 S. U. resistance.
Electro-magnets: 512 convolutions, 5.5 m.m. wire, .3065 S. U. resistance.

Revolutions per minute.	Resistance in S. U.		Reading on electro-dynamometer.	Current in webers.	E. M. F. in volts.	Horse power.			Percentage of energy turned into useful work.
	In outer circuit.	Total in circuit.				Expended.	Total developed.	Developed in outer circuit.	
750	∞					.306			
"	8.9	9.61	1	2.33	20.90	"	.0653	.0605	19.77
"	6.0	6.71	1	"	14.59	"	.0455	.0408	13.33
745	4.5	5.21	1	"	11.33	.304	.0353	.0306	10.00
760	3.5	4.21	7	6.17	24.25	.620	.205	.167	54.93
758	3.25	3.96	16	9.32	34.46	.773	.430	.353	56.90
750	3.0	3.71	26	11.89	41.18	1.224	.656	.531	68.70
740	2.75	3.46	40	14.75	47.65	1.660	.942	.749	61.19
756	2.5	3.20	66	18.95	56.62	2.16	1.44	1.12	67.67
774	2.25	2.96	85	21.50	50.42	2.69	1.71	1.30	60.19
768	2.0	2.71	120	25.55	64.65	3.45	2.21	1.63	60.59
736	1.75	2.46	165	29.96	68.81	3.90	2.76	1.97	57.10
710	1.5	2.21	215	34.20	70.57	4.35	3.23	2.20	56.41
724	1.25	1.96	260	37.61	68.80	5.02	3.47	2.21	50.80
736	1.0	1.71	330	42.37	67.65	6.16	3.84	2.25	44.82
"	.9	1.61	520	53.17	79.92	6.91	5.69	3.16	51.29
"	.8	1.51	570	55.67	78.49	6.91	5.86	3.10	44.87
"	.75	1.46	625	58.31	79.48		6.21	3.19	46.16

No. 6.

Helix: 24 part commutator, 336 convolutions, 2.5 m.m. wire, .4014 S. U. resistance.
Electro-magnets: 512 convolutions, 5.5 m.m. wire, .3065 S. U. resistance.

Revolutions per minute.	Resistance in S. U.		Reading on electro-dyna-mometer.	Current in webers.	E. M. F. in volts.	Horse power.			Percentage of energy turned into useful work.
	In outer circuit.	Total in circuit.				Expended.	Total developed.	Developed in outer circuit.	
500	3.5								
496	3.0	3.71	1.5	2.86	9.90	.257	.0379	.0307	7.58
505	2.5	3.21	2	3.29	9.86	.405	.1434	.0338	6.563
516	2.0	2.71	9	6.99	17.68	.515	.165	.122	21.07
520	1.75	2.46	42	15.11	34.70	.579	.702	.500	62.81
490	1.5	2.21	60	18.06	37.26	.796	.902	.612	51.00
496	1.25	1.96	120	25.55	46.75	1.20	1.61	1.02	56.04
490	1.0	1.71	180	31.30	49.97	1.82	2.09	1.23	53.47
490	.85	1.56	245	36.50	53.16	2.30	2.60	1.42	50.71
504	.75	1.46	280	39.03	53.20	2.80	2.78	1.43	46.42
502	.65	1.36	320	41.72	52.97	3.08	2.96	1.41	45.79
"	.60	1.31	340	43.01	52.60	3.08	3.03	1.39	38.83
"	.55	1.26	355	43.94	51.68	3.58	3.04	1.33	37.15
488	.50	1.21	385	45.76	51.70	3.58	3.17	1.25	34.92
"	.45	1.16	420	47.80	51.77	3.78	3.32	1.29	34.13
"	.40	1.11	491	51.63	53.49	3.98	3.70	1.33	38.42
"	.35	1.06	510	52.66	52.10	4.08	3.68	1.21	29.65
"	.30	1.01	600	57.12	53.89	4.28	4.12	1.22	28.51
"	.25	.96	630	58.54	52.46	4.58	4.11	1.07	23.36

No. 7.

Helix: 24 part commutator, 336 convolutions, 2.5 m.m. wire, .4014 S. U. resistance.
Electro-magnets: 512 convolutions, 5.5 m.m. wire, .3065 S. U. resistance.

Revolutions per minute.	Resistance in S. U.		Reading on electro-dynamometer.	Current in webers.	E. M. F. in volts.	Horse power.			Percentage of energy turned into useful work.
	In outer circuit.	Total in circuit.				Expended.	Total developed.	Developed in outer circuit.	
602	4.5	5.21				.246			
"	3.5	4.21				.491			
590	3.0	3.71	1	2.33	8.07	.602	.0252	.0203	3.372
602	2.5	3.21	16	9.32	27.93	.676	.349	.2725	40.31
606	2.0	2.71	60	18.06	45.69	1.113	1.106	.816	73.81
602	1.75	2.46	105	23.90	54.89	1.72	1.760	1.25	72.67
600	1.5	2.21	140	27.59	56.93	2.20	2.110	1.429	64.95
590	1.25	1.96	170	30.41	55.65	2.53	2.27	1.45	57.31
600	1.0	1.71	270	38.32	61.18	3.43	3.14	1.84	53.64
620	.85	1.56	378	45.34	66.04	4.43	4.01	2.18	49.21
"	.75	1.46	400	46.64	63.57	4.68	3.97	2.05	43.80
"	.60	1.31	505	52.41	64.11	5.06	4.50.	2.06	40.71

No. 8.

Helix: 24 part commutator, 336 convolutions, 2.5 m.m. wire, .4014 S. U. resistance.

Electro-magnets: 512 convolutions, 5.5 m.m. wire, .3065 S. U. resistance.

Revolutions per minute.	Resistance in S. U.		Reading on electro-dyna-mometer.	Current in webers.	E. M. F. in volts.	Horse power.			Percentage of energy turned into useful work.
	In outer circuit.	Total in circuit.				Ex-pended.	Total developed.	Developed in outer circuit.	
715	4.5	5.21			18.32	.365			
698	3.5	4.21	4	4.66	37.03	.427	.114	.095	22.25
700	3.0	3.71	21	10.69	49.42	1.43	.530	.429	30.00
710	2.5	3.21	50	16.49	60.50	1.59	1.09	.682	42.89
680	2.0	2.71	105	23.91	63.11	2.64	1.94	1.43	54.16
690	1.75	2.46	165	29.96	69.75	3.94	2.76	1.98	50.25
708	1.5	2.21	210	33.80	70.13	3.90	3.16	2.14	54.87
685	1.25	1.96	270	38.32	72.58	4.47	3.60	2.30	51.45
686	1.0	1.71	380	45.46	79.66	5.04	4.42	2.59	51.29
720	.85	1.56	550	54.69	79.16	6.46	5.14	3.18	49.22
"	.75	1.46	620	58.07	74.41	6.76	6.16	3.16	46.74
"	.60	1.31	680	60.88	79.05	7.05	6.07	2.78	39.43
"	.50	1.21	900	69.97		7.72	7.42	3.06	39.63

107

No. 9.

Helix: 24 part commutator, 336 convolutions, 2.5 m.m. wire, .4014 S. U. resistance.
Electro-magnets: 512 convolutions, 5.6 m.m. wire, .3065 S. U. resistance.

Revolutions per minute.	Resistance in S.U.		Reading on electro-dynamometer.	Current in webers.	E. M. F. in volts.	Horse power.			Percentage of energy turned into useful work.
	In outer circuit.	Total in circuit.				Expended.	Total Developed.	Developed in outer circuit.	
450	1	1.71	100	23.33	37.24	1.56	1.16	.681	43.65
500	"	"	145	28.08	44.84	2.14	1.69	.987	46.12
550	"	"	190	32.14	51.32	2.69	2.21	1.29	47.95
600	"	"	235	35.75	57.08	3.43	2.73	1.60	46.65
650	"	"	290	39.72	63.42	4.24	3.37	1.97	46.46
700	"	"	360	44.25	70.65	5.00	4.18	2.45	49.00
750	"	"	420	47.80	76.32	5.81	4.89	2.86	49.22
800	"	"	490	51.63	82.44	6.86	5.70	3.34	48.69

No. 10.

Helix: 24 part commutator, 312 convolutions, 2.8 m.m. wire, .234 S. U. resistance.
Electro-magnets: 3200 convolutions, 2.8 m.m. wire, 7 563 S. U. resistance.

Revolutions per minute.	Resistance in S. U.		Reading on electro-dynamometer.			Current in webers.			F. M. F. in helix in volts.	Horse power.			Percentage of energy turned into useful work.
	In outer circuit.	Total in circuit.	Helix.	Electro-magnet.	Outer circuit.	Helix.	Electro-magnet.	Outer circuit.		Expended.	Total developed.	Developed in outer circuit.	
502	8	7.8	13	13	...	8.41	8.41	...	61.25	1.33	.69	...	27.82
513	12.0	4.87	30	12	5	12.77	8.08	5.21	58.07	1.47	.994	.409	30.12
517	10.0	4.54	35	12	7	13.80	8.08	6.17	58.50	1.58	1.082	.476	34.72
520	9.0	4.34	42	12	9	15.11	8.08	7.0	61.23	1.59	1.251	.552	35.90
498	7.5	3.99	40	10	10	14.75	7.37	7.37	54.95	1.42	1.086	.510	40.00
501	5.0	3.51	42	8	15	15.11	6.60	9.03	50.36	1.53	1.020	.612	44.05
500	4.5	3.05	50	7	22	16.49	6.17	10.94	46.96	1.53	1.098	.674	47.12
510	3.5	2.62	75	7	35	20.20	6.17	13.8	49.41	1.77	1.338	.834	49.25
502	3.0	2.38	82	6	42	21.12	5.71	15.11	46.93	1.74	1.329	.857	45.75
507	2.5	2.11	90	6	50	22.12	5.71	16.49	43.58	1.86	1.292	.851	56.92
502	2.0	1.81	120	6	85	25.55	5.71	21.5	43.18	1.95	1.479	1.11	58.85
495	1.75	1.65	140	5	95	27.59	5.21	22.73	42.5	1.92	1.572	1.13	55.72
492	1.5	1.48	160	4	110	29.50	4.66	24.46	40.77	2.01	1.612	1.12	55.09
504	1.25	1.30	190	4	140	32.14	4.66	27.59	39.01	2.16	1.681	1.19	51.10
506	1.1	1.19	205	4	157	33.89	4.66	29.21	37.12	2.27	1.661	1.16	50.23
512	1.0	1.11	200	4	155	32.98	4.66	29.03	34.18	2.09	1.511	1.05	53.06
505	.85	.998	225	4	180	34.98	4.66	31.30	32.60	1.96	1.528	1.04	49.95
510	.75	.917	220	4	183	34.60	4.66	31.55	29.63	1.87	1.374	.934	38.79
507	.6	.790	160	3	120	29.50	4.04	25.55	21.77	1.45	.861	.490	

No. 11.

Helix: 24 part commutator, 312 convolutions, 2.8 m.m. wire, .234 S. U. resistance.
Electro-magnets: 3200 convolutions, 2.8 m.m. wire, 7.563 S. U. resistance.

Revolutions per minute.	Resistance in S. U.		Reading on electro-dynamometer.			Current in webers.			E. M. F. in helix in volts.	Horse power.			Percentage of energy turned into useful work.
	In outer circuit.	Total in circuit.	Helix.	Electro-magnet.	Outer circuit.	Helix.	Electro-magnet.	Outer circuit.		Expended.	Total developed.	Developed in outer circuit.	
594	.3	.52	3	1	3	4.04	2.33	4.04	1.962	.24	.0106	.00019	2.654
596	.4	.61	4	1	3	4.66	2.33	4.04	2.655	.24	.0166	.00017	3.404
612	.5	.70	30	1	26	12.77	2.33	11.89	8.34	.375	.143	.0884	23.57
"	.6	.79	180	2	...	31.30	3.30		23.08		.968		
620	.6	.79	215	2	180	34.20	3.30	31.30	25.23	.87	1.16	.736	41.68
615	.7	.87	280	3	240	39.03	4.04	36.14	31.71	1.77	1.66	1.14	50.44
"	.75	.917	300	4	250	40.40	4.66	36.88	34.59	2.26	1.87	1.28	51.50
600	.85	.998	290	4	245	39.72	4.66	36.50	37.02	2.51	1.97	1.42	55.25
612	1.0	1.11	305	6	235	40.73	5.71	35.75	42.21	2.571	2.30	1.60	55.74
"	1.25	1.30	290	7	210	39.72	6.17	33.80	48.22	2.87	2.56	1.80	62.98
598	1.5	1.48	230	8	160	35.37	6.60	29.50	48.88	2.89	2.32	1.63	58.00
615	2.0	1.81	195	10	120	32.57	7.34	25.55	55.05	2.81	2.40	1.63	56.40
620	3.0	2.38	130	12	65	26.58	8.08	18.80	59.07	2.66	2.10	1.33	50.00
625	4.5	3.05	85	14	32	21.50	8.88	13.10	61.23	2.30	1.76	.98	42.61
"	6.0	3.59	70	15	22	19.51	9.03	10.94	65.40	2.16	1.71	.898	41.57
620	7.5	3.99	55	16	16	17.29	9.33	9.33	64.42	1.89	1.49	.817	42.22

No. 12.

Helix: 24 part commutator, 312 convolutions, 2.8 m.m. wire, .234 S. U. resistance.
Electro-magnets: 3200 convolutions, 2.8 m.m. wire, 7.563 S. U. resistance.

Revolutions per minute.	Resistance in S. U.		Reading on electro-dynamometer.			Current in webers.			E. M. F. in helix in volts.	Horse power.			Percentage of energy turned into useful work.
	In outer circuit.	Total in circuit.	Helix.	Electro-magnet.	Outer circuit.	Helix.	Electro-magnet.	Outer circuit.		Expended.	Total developed.	Developed in outer circuit.	
700	7.5	4.01	80	18	18	20.86	9.89	9.89	78.10	2.57	2.18	.918	35.72
"	6.0	3.59	80	17	25	20.86	9.62	11.68	69.92	2.57	1.95	1.02	39.69
707	4.5	3.06	95	16	35	22.73	9.33	13.80	64.94	2.88	1.97	1.07	37.15
710	3.0	2.39	165	14	90	29.96	8.88	22.12	66.85	3.19	2.68	1.84	57.67
704	2.5	2.12	195	12	115	32.57	8.08	25.01	64.47	3.59	2.81	1.96	54.59
716	2.0	1.82	235	9	150	35.75	7.0	28.56	60.75	3.94	2.91	2.04	51.77
723	1.5	1.49	315	7	220	41.40	6.17	34.60	57.60	4.28	3.20	2.25	52.57
715	1.25	1.31	350	6	260	43.64	5.71	37.61	53.38	4.23	3.12	2.21	52.25
722	1.0	1.12	385	5	300	45.76	5.21	40.40	47.85	4.27	2.93	2.04	47.77
705	.75	.92	370	5	305	44.86	5.21	40.73	38.53	3.45	2.31	1.56	45.21
703	.60	.80	300	5	270	40.40	5.21	38.32	30.18	2.20	1.63	1.10	48.03
716	.50	.71	150	4	100	28.56	4.66	23.32	18.94	.292	.725	.34	11.64
710	.40	.62	7	1	7	6.17	2.3	6.17	3.571	.290	.295	.019	6.552

No. 13.

Helix: 24 part commutator, 312 convolutions, 2.8 m.m. wire, .234 S. U. resistance.

Electro-magnets: 3200 convolutions, 2.8 m.m. wire, 7.563 S. U. resistance.

Revolutions per minute.	Resistance in S. U.		Reading on electro-dynamometer.			Current in webers.			E. M. F. in helix in volts.	Horse power.			Percentage of energy turned into useful work.
	In outer circuit.	Total in circuit.	Helix.	Electro-magnet.	Outer circuit.	Helix.	Electro-magnet.	Outer circuit.		Expended.	Total developed.	Developed in outer circuit.	
450	1.0	1.12	140		105	27.59		23.91	28.85	1.47	1.02	.715	48.63
500	"	"	185		150	31.72		28.56	33.16	1.94	1.41	1.02	52.57
550	"	"	250		195	36.88		32.57	38.56	2.47	1.91	1.33	53.85
600	"	"	325		260	42.05		37.61	43.97	3.06	2.48	1.77	57.84
650	"	"	400		305	46.04		40.73	48.77	3.71	3.05	2.08	56.06
700	"	"	470		350	50.56		43.64	52.87	4.43	3.58	2.38	53.72
750	"	"	530		395	53.69		46.35	56.14	5.20	3.91	2.69	51.73
800	"	"	640		460	58.98		50.03	61.69	5.88	4.86	3.13	53.23
850	"	"	700		510	61.69		52.66	64.51	6.42	5.33	3.47	54.05
900	"	"	785		570	65.33		55.67	68.31	6.98	5.98	3.88	55.59
850	"	"	700		505	61.09		52.41	64.51	6.42	5.33	3.44	53.58
800	"	"	600		440	57.12		48.92	59.73	5.71	4.57	2.99	52.38
750	"	"	510		372	52.66		44.98	55.07	4.90	3.89	2.53	51.63
700	"	"	440		330	48.92		42.37	51.15	4.14	3.35	2.25	54.35
650	"	"	350		270	43.64		38.32	45.63	3.45	3.07	1.84	53.33
600	"	"	285		220	39.47		34.60	41.27	2.82	2.18	1.5	53.19
550	"	"	240		180	36.14		31.30	37.79	2.24	1.83	1.23	54.91
500	"	"	180		135	31.30		27.09	32.73	1.73	1.37	.918	53.06
450	"	"	135		100	27.09		23.32	28.33	1.28	1.03	.681	53.20

No. 14.

Helix: 24 part commutator, 312 convolutions, 2.8 m.m. wire, .234 S. U. resistance.
Electro-magnets: 2240 convolutions, 3 m.m. wire, 4.46 S. U. resistance.

Revolutions per minute.	Resistance in S. U.		Reading on electro-dynamometer.			Current in webers.			E. M. F. in helix in volts.	Horse power.			Percentage of energy turned into useful work.
	In outer circuit.	Total in circuit.	Helix.	Electro-magnet.	Outer circuit.	Helix.	Electro-magnet.	Outer circuit.		Expended.	Total developed.	Developed in outer circuit.	
505	8.0	4.70	28	28		11.19	11.19		49.01	1.34	.736		
510	7.0	2.96	55		9	17.29		6.99	47.79	1.77	1.11	.428	24.18
502	6.0	2.8	60		12	18.06		8.08	47.21	1.74	1.14	.490	28.16
502	5.0	2.6	65	18	14	18.80	9.89	8.88	45.64	1.74	1.15	.493	28.38
492	4.5	2.48	65	16	16	18.80	9.33	9.32	48.53	1.71	1.10	.489	28.60
"	3.0	2.03	120	15	40	25.55	9.03	14.75	48.43	1.71	1.66	.817	47.78
515	2.5	1.84	125	14	53	26.07	8.88	16.98	44.79	1.99	1.57	.902	45.82
494	2.0	1.62	145	13	7	28.08	8.40	19.51	42.47	1.91	1.60	.953	49.89
"	1.5	1.36	180	10	100	31.20	7.37	23.32	39.75	2.01	1.67	1.02	50.74
508	1.25	1.22	210		130	33.80		26.58	38.50	2.18	1.74	1.10	50.46
512	1.0	1.06	260	9	170	37.61	6.90	30.41	32.73	2.40	1.65	1.16	48.83
515	1.0	1.06	280		180	39.03		31.30	38.65	2.41	2.02	1.23	51.08
508	1.0	.99	295		205	40.06		33.39	36.93	2.37	1.98	1.25	52.74
515	.9	.92	220	7	220	34.60	6.17	34.60	29.72	2.52	1.38	1.20	47.61
"	.8	.84	295		222	40.06		34.75	31.42	2.52	1.69	1.05	41.67
498	.3	.52	95	2	75	22.73	3.29	20.20	11.04	0.71	.336	.153	21.55
510	.6	.77	280	5	200	39.03	5.21	32.98	28.06	2.18	1.47	.817	37.48
"	.5	.69	275		210	38.68		33.80	24.92	2.42	1.29	.715	29.54

No. 15.

Helix: 24 part commutator, 312 convolutions, 2.8 m.m. wire, .234 S. U. resistance.
Electro-magnets: 2240 convolutions, 3 m.m. wire, 4.46 S. U. resistance.

Revolutions per minute.	Resistance in S. U.		Reading on electro-dynamometer.			Current in webers.			E. M. F. in helix in volts.	Horse power.			Percentage of energy turned into useful work.
	In outer circuit.	Total in circuit.	Helix.	Electro-magnet.	Outer circuit.	Helix.	Electro-magnet.	Outer circuit.		Expended.	Total developed.	Developed in outer circuit.	
700	.1	.24				3.29			1.044	.24	.0046		
	.2	.31	3			4.03			1.617	.24	.0087	.0204	
	.3	.43	3		10	8.88		7.37	4.311	.24	.0518	.0326	7.034
712	.4	.52	14	4	12	9.03	4.66	8.07	5.143	.29	.0622	1.04	11.64
698	.5	.61	15	6	305	44.86	5.71	40.73	28.89	.26	1.74	1.51	39.84
712	.6	.69	370		370	52.66		41.86	37.86	2.61	2.67	1.83	43.14
715	.75	.77	510	15	360	55.67	9.03	44.25	45.74	3.50	3.41	2.28	44.85
720	1.0	.88	570	18	335	53.69	9.80	42.69	53.14	4.08	3.82	2.21	55.61
714	1.25	1.06	630	21	260	48.93	10.69	37.61	55.73	4.10	3.66	2.20	54.16
708	1.5	1.22	440	25	215	47.23	11.08	34.20	59.97	4.08	3.80	2.04	54.32
700	2.0	1.36	410	32	150	42.05	13.19	28.56	63.60	4.00	3.18	1.63	51.00
712	3.0	1.62	325	50	80	35.37	16.65	20.86	67.04	3.48			46.83
	∞	2.03	230							2.47			
		4.7											

No. 16.

Helix: 24 part commutator, 288 convolutions, 3 m.m. wire, .173 S. U. resistance.
Electro-magnets: 3916 convolutions, 2.5 m.m. wire, 11.26 S. U. resistance.

Revolutions per minute.	Resistance in S. U.		Reading on electro-dynamometer.			Current in webers.			E. M. F. in helix in volts.	Horse power.			Percentage of energy turned into useful work.
	In outer circuit.	Total in circuit.	Helix.	Electro-magnet.	Outer circuit.	Helix.	Electro-magnet.	Outer circuit.		Expended.	Total developed.	Developed in outer circuit.	
612	0.0	.118								.25			
640	.25	.052								.25			
635	.5	.870	45			4.66			2.84	.25	.018		60.6
620	.75	1.09	295	2.0	90.0	22.97	3.3	22.12	18.8	.76	.579	.46	52.86
630	1.0	1.29	220	8.0	190.0	34.6	4.04	32.14	35.21	2.44	1.63	1.29	62.64
630	1.25	1.5	225	3.5	190.0	34.98	4.36	32.14	11.13	2.57	1.93	1.61	66.79
635	1.5	1.69	205	3.5	170.0	33.39	4.30	30.41	46.76	2.59	2.09	1.3	70.32
636	1.75	1.87	185	4.0	145.0	31.72	4.66	28.08	50.05	2.46	2.13	1.73	75.99
638	2.0	2.88	165	6.0	120.0	29.96	5.71	25.55	52.3	2.47	2.10	1.63	65.90
628	4.5	4.29	68	6.0	82.0	20.23	6.16	13.19	60.09	2.05	1.56	.98	47.88
624	6.5	6.17	42	7.5	15.0	15.11	6.39	9.03	60.52	1.91	1.22	.66	34.55
635	9.0	5.73	32	7.0	8.5	13.19	6.16	6.8	63.07	1.81	1.13	.521	28.78
610	11.0	11.43	25	8.0	7.0	11.68	6.16	6.16	62.49	1.62	.98	.522	32.32
614	∞		8			6.6	6.6		70.43	1.25	.629		

No. 17.

Helix: 24 part commutator, 288 convolutions, 3 m.m. wire, .173 S. U. resistance.

Electro-magnets: 3916 convolutions, 2.5 m.m. wire, 11.26 S. U. resistance.

Revolutions per minute.	Resistance in S. U.		Reading on electro-dynamometer.			Current in webers.			E. M. F. in helix in volts.	Horse power.			Percentage of energy turned into useful work
	In outer circuit.	Total in circuit.	Helix.	Electro-magnet.	Outer circuit.	Helix.	Electro-magnet.	Outer circuit.		Expended.	Total developed.	Developed in outer circuit.	
685	.25	.42	3		3	4.01		4.04	1.58	.271	.0085	.0051	1.82
670	.5	.652	30		28	12.77		12.31	7.74	.547	.182	.095	17.37
665	.75	.875	245	2.0	225	36.50	3.3	34.98	29.85	2.04	1.45	1.14	55.88
640	.85	.963	255	2.5	235	37.25	3.69	35.75	33.49	2.29	1.67	1.86	59.98
640	1.0	1.09	290	3.0	260	39.72	4.04	37.61	40.43	2.61	2.15	1.77	67.81
645	1.1	1.17	250	3.5	230	38.47	4.04	35.37	42.02	2.63	2.17	1.72	65.40
650	1.25	1.29	272	4.0	205	36.88	4.36	33.39	44.42	2.65	2.2	1.74	65.66
645	1.4	1.42	235	4.0	185	35.75	4.06	31.72	47.39	2.63	2.57	1.76	66.92
650	1.5	1.5	225	4.5	180	35.22	4.06	31.3	49.33	2.52	2.33	1.84	73.01
660	1.75	1.69	200	5.0	153	32.98	4.94	28.84	52.04	2.56	2.3	1.82	71.09
680	2.0	1.87	180		145	31.3	5.21	28.08	54.65	2.42	2.29	1.07	81.40

No. 18.

Helix · 25 parts commutator, 278 convolutions, 3 m.m. wire, .173 S. U. resistance.
Electro-magnets : 3,916 convolutions, 2.5 m.m. wire, 11 26 S. U. resistance.

Revolutions per minute.	Resistance in S.U.		Reading on electro-dynamometer.			Current in webers.			E. M. F. in helix in volts.	Horse power.			Percentage of energy turned into useful work.
	In outer circuit.	Total in circuit.	Helix.	Electro-magnet.	Outer circuit.	Helix.	Electro-magnet.	Outer circuit.		Expended.	Total developed.	Developed in outer circuit.	
817	1.1	1.17	435	..	360	48.65	..	44.25	53.15	4.67	3.47	2.69	57.6
812	1.0	1.09	465	..	385	50.29	5.21	45.76	51.11	4.81	3.44	2.61	54.26
815	1.25	1.29	405	5.0	335	46.94	5.47	42.69	56.53	4.82	3.56	2.85	59.12
820	1.5	1.5	370	5.5	290	44.86	..	39.72	62.88	4.85	3.78	2.96	61.08
814	1.75	1.69	330	..	250	42.37	..	36.88	66.85	4.82	3.8	2.98	61.82
812	2.0	1.87	300	..	220	40.40	..	34.6	70.54	4.64	3.82	3.00	64.65
824	.9	1.01	450	..	385	49.47	..	45.76	46.65	4.71	3.69	2.36	50.10
820	.8	.92	450	..	390	49.47	..	46.06	42.56	4.35	2.82	2.12	48.73
808	.75	.876	430	..	390	48.36	..	46.06	39.55	4.12	2.56	1.99	48.30
840	.6	.743	220	..	215	34.60	..	34.2	24.00	2.4	1.11	.878	36.58
830	.5	.652	..	..	100	..	..	23.32	..	2.37	..	.34	14.34
820	.5	.652	75	..	70	20.20	..	19.51	12.30	2.34	.333	.238	10.16

No. 19.

Helix : 24 part commutator, 288 convolutioos, 3 m. m. wire, .173 S. U. resistance.

Electro-magnets : 3916 convolutions, 2.5 m.m. wire, 11.26 S. U. resistance.

Revolutions per minute.	Resistance in S. U.		Reading on electro-dynamometer.			Current in webers.			E. M. F. in helix in volts.	Horse power.			Percentage of energy turned into useful work.
	In outer circuit.	Total in circuit.	Helix.	Electro-magnet.	Outer circuit.	Helix.	Electro-magnet.	Outer circuit.		Expended.	Total developed.	Developed in outer circuit.	
480	1.0	1.091	98	....	85	23.09	....	21.5	23.53	1.37	.728	.578	42.19
530	"	"	135	....	123	27.09	....	25.86	27.60	1.73	1.00	.837	46.38
602	"	"	223	....	195	34.83	....	32.57	35.49	2.33	1.65	1.33	57.08
670	"	"	290	....	250	39.72	....	36.88	40.47	3.14	2.15	1.7	54.14
744	"	"	300	....	320	46.06	....	41.72	46.93	3.95	2.89	2.18	55.19
800	"	"	455	....	380	49.75	....	45.46	50.70	4.73	3.38	2.59	54.76
864	"	"	515	....	430	52.92	....	48.36	53.92	5.64	3.82	2.93	51.95
911	"	"	585	....	490	56.42	....	51.03	57.49	6.32	4.35	3.34	52.86

No. 20.

Helix : 24 part commutator, 288 convolutions, 3 m.m. wire, .173 S. U. resistance.
Electro-magnets : 3,200 convolutions, 2.8 m.m. wire, 7,563 U. S. resistance.

Revolutions per minute.	Resistance in U.S.		Reading on electro-dynamometer.			Current in webers.			E. M. F. in helix in volts.	Horse power.			Percentage of energy turned into useful work.
	Outer circuit.	Total in circuit.	Helix.	Electro-magnet.	Outer circuit.	Helix.	Electro-magnet.	Outer circuit.		Expended.	Total developed.	Developed in outer circuit.	
716	8	7.74	26	26.0		11.89	11.89	32.57	85.93	2.04	1.37	2.66	78.48
710	2.0	1.75	300	15.0	195	40.4	9.03	34.6	66.01	3.62	3.57	2.62	70.05
706	1.75	1.59	320	13.5	220	41.72	8.57	37.25	61.93	3.74	3.46	2.61	65.91
718	1.5	1.42	360	12.0	255	44.25	8.08	39.72	58.66	3.96	3.48	2.47	60.84
710	1.25	1.25	395	9.0	290	46.35	6.99	43.01	54.10	4.06	3.36	2.31	57.18
708	1.0	1.00	445	7.0	340	49.21	6.16	44.25	48.70	4.04	3.21	2.38	61.47
714	.95	1.02	460	6.0	360	50.03	5.71	44.86	47.65	3.79	3.2	2.27	60.53
706	.9	.977	460		360	50.03		45.46	45.64	3.62	3.19	2.07	57.18
710	.8	.896	460	5.0	370	50.23	5.21	45.16	41.85	3.75	2.81	1.78	53.13
714	.7	.814	445	4.0	380	49.20	4.66	43.01	37.40	3.62	2.47	1.39	50.18
715	.6	.729	390		375	46.06		85.37	31.35	3.35	1.94	.875	
715	.5	.642			340	33.39		32.57		2.77		.665	
710	.5	.642	205		230 195				20.02	1.3	.896		51.15

No. 21.

Helix: 24 part commutator, 288 convolutions, 3 m.m. wire, .173 S. U. resistance.
Electro-magnets: 3200 convolutions, 2.8 m.m. wire, 7.563 S. U. resistance.

Revolutions per minute.	Resistance in S. U.		Reading on electro-dynamometer.			Current on webers.			E. M. F. in helix in volts.	Horse power.			Percentage of energy turned into useful work.
	Outer circuit.	Total in circuit.	Helix.	Electro-magnet.	Outer circuit.	Helix.	Electro-magnet.	Outer circuit.		Expended.	Total developed.	Developed in outer circuit.	
468	1.0	1.06	170	...	130	30.41	...	26.58	30.10	1.34	1.23	.884	65.97
532	"	"	235	...	185	35.75	...	31.72	35.38	1.96	1.69	1.26	64.21
610	"	"	310	...	240	41.06	...	36.14	40.64	2.61	2.24	1.64	62.83
678	"	"	365	...	290	44.56	...	30.72	44.10	3.32	2.63	1.98	59.64
716	"	"	430	...	335	48.36	...	42.68	47.86	3.79	3.10	2.28	60.16
788	"	"	510	...	385	52.66	...	45.76	52.12	4.35	3.67	2.63	60.40
860	"	"	620	...	430	57.14	...	48.36	56.55	5.08	4.33	2.93	57.68

No. 22.

Helix: 24 part commutator, 288 convolutions, 3 m.m. wire, .173 S. U. resistance.
Electro-magnets: 2556 convolutions, 3 m.m. wire, 4.46 S. U. resistance.

Revolutions per minute.	Resistance in S. U.		Reading on electro-dynamometer.			Current in webers.			E. M. F. in helix in volts.	Horse power.			Percentage of energy turned into useful work.
	In outer circuit.	Total in circuit.	Helix.	Electro-magnet.	Outer circuit.	Helix.	Electro-magnet.	Outer circuit.		Expended.	Total developed.	Developed in outer circuit.	
690	8	4.63	46	46		15.82	15.82		68.4	2.67	1.45	2.11	52.62
702	2.0	1.55	300	24	155	40.4	11.43	29.03	58.47	4.01	3.16	2.03	51.13
694	1.75	1.43	300	22	170	40.4	10.94	30.41	53.94	3.97	2.92	2.09	52.38
698	1.5	1.29	335	20	205	42.69	10.43	33.39	51.42	3.99	2.94	2.08	50.48
696	1.25	1.15	390	18	245	46.06	9.9	36.50	49.46	4.12	3.06	1.8	45.22
696	1.0	.99	395	14	265	46.35	8.88	37.97	42.85	3.98	2.67	1.78	50.57
690	.9	.92	390	9	290	46.06	6.99	39.72	39.50	3.52	2.44	1.58	46.61
649	.8	.85	385	8	290	45.75	6.6	39.72	36.82	3.89	2.22	1.29	42.71
706	.7	.78	360	7	270	44.25	6.16	38.32	32.14	3.02	1.9	1.0	37.73
684	.5	.702	290		245	39.72		36.50	28.02	2.65	1.38	.544	43.18
684	.5	.623			160			29.50		1.26			
		.623	140			27.59			16.05	1.26	.594		

No. 23.

Helix: 24 part commutator, 288 convolutions, 3 m.m. wire, .173 S. U. resistance.
Electro-magnets, 2556 convolutions. 3 m.m. wire, 4.46 S. U. resistance.

Revolutions per minute.	Resistance in S.U.		Reading on electro-dynamometer.			Current in webers.			E.M.F. in helix in volts.	Horse power.			Percentage of energy turned into useful work.
	Outer circuit.	Total in circuit.	Helix.	Electro-magnet.	Outer circuit.	Helix.	Electro-magnet.	Outer circuit.		Expended.	Total developed.	Developed in outer circuit.	
492	1	.99	240	7.0	160	36.14	6.16	29.5	33.41	2.11	1.62	1.09	51.66
528	"	"	282	9.0	185	39.17	6.99	31.72	31.21	2.48	1.9	1.26	50.81
602	"	"	345	12.0	235	43.31	8.08	35.75	40.04	3.07	2.32	1.0	52.12
634	"	"	410	14.0	280	47.23	8.88	39.03	43.66	3.61	2.70	1.9	52.63
722	"	"	450	16.0	300	49.47	9.88	40.4	45.73	4.27	3.03	2.04	47.78
790	"	"	540	18.5	385	54.20	10.08	42.69	50.10	5.0	3.64	2.28	45.60
856	"	"	610	21.0	370	57.60	10.09	44.86	53.24	5.76	4.11	2.52	48.74

ELECTRIC LIGHTING

AT THE

PARIS EXHIBITION.

By WILLIAM HENRY PREECE, F. R. S.

From the "Journal of the Society of Arts."

Electric Lighting at the Paris Exhibition.

THE recent International Exhibition of Electricity in Paris makes an epoch in the history of the practical applications of that science to Arts, Manufactures, and Commerce. I purpose now to refer only to its application to artificial illumination; but there are many other branches fully deserving examination and discussion by this Society. It was, however, as an exhibition of electric lighting that it was principally attractive, and those who saw it for the first time will never forget the vivid impression that the great blaze of splendor produced upon their minds on entering the building. There never can be anything like it again, for as wisdom grows with experience, so no manager of any future Exhibition is likely to repeat that terrific *mélange* of lights that flooded the interior of the Palais de l'Industrie with great brilliancy, but with an impracticable and impossible means of comparing and judging the relative merits of different systems.

For instance, at the forthcoming Exhibition at the Crystal Palace, the building—splendidly adapted for the purpose—will be divided into sections, each section being lit by one, and only one system. But at Paris, Pelion was piled upon Ossa; the British Section, for instance, received rays from at least a dozen different sources. To estimate the value of a Siemens lamp you had to eliminate the disturbing influence of a blazing Crompton; and to admire the star-like Jaspar arc, you had to run the gauntlet of a flock of Swans. The fretful Jamin, or the fitful Jablochkoff, was masked by the steady Gülcher or the brilliant Serrin. In the galleries, however, it was different. Here, different *salles* were illuminated by different systems; a small theatre was lit by the Werderman lamp, and a picture gallery most effectively shown up by the *Lampe*

Soleil; a buffet was softly and brightly lit up with the Swan lamp, while Mr. Edison's numerous exhibits, in his own *salons,* were as visible by night as by day, thanks to his own beautiful lamp.

It is not my intention to examine, *seriatim,* the various machines, lamps, and modes of illumination shown. With most of them, you are already familiar. But I purpose to select what appeared to me to be novelties, and what seemed worthy of being brought to your notice, as steps in advance.

On the night of August 29th, there were in operation 277 arc lamps, 116 candles, 44 arc incandescent lamps, 1,500 incandescent lamps, or a total of 1,837 electric lights in all, at the Paris Exhibition. Towards the end of the period during which the show was opened, this number was very largely increased, and I have little doubt that the number reached 2,500 in the beginning of November. Now this army of lamps required power to convert the energy stored up in coal into energy of motion: dynamo - ma-

chines to convert the energy of motion
into electrical energy; conductors to
transport this electric energy to the point
to be illuminated: lamps to convert the
electric energy into energy of heat, and
therefore of light.

The exhibition of engines and machinery was very extensive, although our
English manufacturers failed to do what
they might have done had they thought
as highly of the Exhibition at first as they
did afterwards. Many of our manufacturers were conspicuous by their absence.
The only extensive display was by Messrs.
Robey & Co., of Lincoln, who showed
eight of their well-known engines, with a
total power of 250 horses, and I have
every reason to believe that their success
has amply repaid them for their enter-
prise. Mr. Brotherhood made a small
show of his well-known three-cylinder
engines and Messrs. Wallis & Stevens, of
Basingstoke, sent one of their semi-fixed
steam-engines, with their pretty and effective governor for adjusting the speed
while in motion—uniformity in speed be-

ing an essential criterion of an electric light engine. The foreigners, for a wonder, far outshone the British in the magnitude of their displays.

One of the most valuable exhibits was made by Messrs. Thomson, Sterne & Co., who showed a new gas engine on a new principle, which attracted a great deal of attention. Gas is destined to play a most important *rôle* in the future of electric lighting. Its function is that of a heat-generator. The energy of the coal exists in gas in a form which can develop more light, when converted into the form of electricity, by the current, than in the form of heat by combustion. Gas engines have a very high theoretical efficiency, and they are free from the dangers of boilers, the neglect of stokers, or the waste of energy in chimneys.

Gas engines on the " Otto " principle, from half horse power to 50-horse power, were very extensively exhibited by France, but the machine of Thomson, Sterne & Co. (Clerk's patent) excelled them all in lightness, compactness, regularity, and safety. One of these engines may now be seen at work at the Smoke Abatement Exhibition at South Kensington, and several have been ordered ·for private houses. As an adjunct to the gas engine, Mr. Dowson exhibited an interesting and valuable process of making cheap gas for motor purposes. Prof. Ayrton reported that in a series of trials made with a $3\frac{1}{2}$ H. P. (nominal) "Otto" engine, driven by the Dowson gas, one H. P. (indicated) was obtained per hour by the consumption of gas derived from 1.46 lbs. of coal. For larger engines he anticipated a consumption of only 1.2 lbs. per indicated horse power per hour. You will have a paper during the Session by Mr. Dowson himself, describing his mode of manufacture. When perhaps 6 lbs. of coal per horse power per hour are consumed in the present electric-light steam-engines, you can form some idea of the economy to be effected by cheap gas.

Dynamo - machines — machines which convert the energy of motion into electrical energy, through the medium of magnetism—were exhibited in abundance, of all kinds and forms, from the original apparatus of Faraday, made with his own hands, to Mr. Edison's latest development of this wonderful source of electric currents. There are two kinds of machines—the one producing currents from fixed and permanent steel magnets, the other from electro-magnets, excited by the currents which they themselves generate. Each kind is also sub-divided into two others, in one of which continuous currents are produced, flowing in one direction, called the *continuous current machine;* and in the other alternate currents, called the *alternate current machine,* where the current rapidly reverses and changes its direction. The production of currents by these machines is due to the simple fact discovered by Faraday, that if a conductor, such as a copper wire, be moved rapidly through a magnetized space, or a magnetic field, as it is called, this conductor is electrified so that, if its two ends be connected, a current flows. The intensity of this current depends, first, on the intensity of the magnetism present, on the velocity with which the conductor moves through the field, and on the direction with which it cuts the lines of magnetic force which permeate the magnetic field. The magneto-electric kind—the manufacture and invention of M. de Meritens—are very much approved of by our Trinity House for lighthouse purposes, and a very fine display of them was made by M. de Meritens, who seemed to live in the Exhibition, for he was always there, and who never seemed to tire of giving his clear and able descriptions. He exhibited alternate and continuous current machines, and he richly deserved the gold medal that was accorded to him. The exhibition of dynamo-machines was rendered very interesting by the exhibition of an early machine of Elias, of Haarlem, of 1842, and of Pacinotti's machines of 1861. The former was shown in the Dutch Section, and the latter in the Italian. Here we have the germs of all the present machines, and by whatever name a machine may be known, it can be traced back to these original types. The Pacinotti apparatus has been very greatly improved by Gramme, and by Siemens—forms well known to every one—but it has received its greatest development in the Edison machine, which was one of the wonders of the Exhibition. As this was one of the greatest novelties, I must briefly describe it. In the first place, I must point out that the machine is larger than any one that has ever been made before. It weighs, with engine and bed plates, 20 tons, and it can produce a current of electricity of nearly 900 amperes.* As the largest machine of the Gramme type weighs scarcely one ton, and produces a current of but 93 amperes, the difference becomes striking. Now, Mr. Edison has struck out three new paths, first—in the bulk and form of his electro-magnets, second—in the size and construction of his armature, and third—in the low resistance of his revolving coil. By the

---

*The largest Brush machine weighs two tons, and absorbs 40-horse power.

first, he secures an intense and concentrated magnetic field, by the second he secures a high cutting velocity for the moving conductor through this field, and by the third, he secures a very powerful current to be distributed among a great number of lamps with the least possible waste of energy. The long and bulky coils, 8 feet long, which constitute his electro-magnet, have excited the surprise of many electricians, but there is no doubt that he has arrived at this form after many careful practical experiments, supported by the mathematical investigations of Professor Rowland—a very high authority—and that the result is to obtain an intense field in a large space, with the least absorption of electrical energy in the coils. With 350 revolutions per minute he is able to produce an electro-motive force of 110 volts, which an ordinary Gramme machine can only attain with over 1,000 revolutions per minute. His field-magnets are wound with copper wire, which have a resistance of 30 ohms. and which are connected as a

shunt to the main circuit, as was origi
nally done by Wheatstone, and is now
followed by Dr. Siemens and Sir William
Thomson. The armature is not wound
with wire, but is constructed with solid
bars of copper $\frac{3}{4}$ in. by $\frac{1}{2}$ in. section, and
$3\frac{1}{4}$ feet long, which are well insulated
from each other, and are most ingeniously
connected at their ends by copper discs,
so that all the bars, of which there are
138, form one continuous circuit, whose
total resistance is only 0.008 of an ohm.
The diameter of the armature is 28 inches.
The core of the armature is made up of
1,700 thin iron discs insulated from each
other by paper, and well clamped into a
solid mass by bolts. This is done to
avoid the heating effects due to so-called
Foucault currents induced in the metal
and absorbing or wasting energy. The
iron core of the armature becomes thus
magnetized, and it concentrates the field
to the space through which the conductor
moves, as is done in Siemens' and other
machines.

There are two great troubles in exist·

ing machines, want of uniformity in their motion and the slipping of belts. The former is met by governors, and the latter by direct gearing. Steadiness of motion is most essential, otherwise we have that painful throbbing of the light that is so irritating to the eyes. Mr. Edison connects his armature direct to his steam motor, which is a high-pressure engine of the Allen-Porter type, governed by an ingenious centrifugal regulator, and rotating very uniformly at 350 revolutions per minute, without any multiplying gear whatever. When the machine is giving out its maximum commercial effect it absorbes 125-horse power, the external resistance should be 16 times that of the armature, the electro-motive force 110 volts, and the current consequently 860 amperes. It is not safe to exceed this limit, for the armature then becomes unduly heated. A special blower is added to direct cold air on the armature to keep down the heat, when the work of the machine approaches its limit. The brush is a special feature of the machine. The

absence of sparking was very striking.
Mr. Edison coats his brush and commutator with an amalgam of copper, which
diminishes the electrical resistance of
contact, reduces the heat, and prevents
sparking.

Those who are interested in this machine—and every one should be, for it is
a decided step in advance—will soon have
an opportunity of seeing it at work at 57,
High Holborn.

There was a very interesting form of
Gramme machine shown, which was maintained at a velocity of 2,400 revolutions
per minute, and was said to generate an
electromotive force of 2,000 volts. It
maintained 60 Jamin candles alight. But
one of the best and most compact forms
of Gramme was that shown by the British Electric Light Company, designed by
their engineer, and made for them by
Messrs. Emerson, in Stockport.

The display of lamps was the display
of the building. There were very few
novelties among arc lamps. An arc lamp
consists of two sticks or rods of carbon,

which are kept apart a small fraction of
an inch while the current flows through
them, but which comes together when
the current ceases. Across the interval
separating them there is a steady flow of
electricity, accompanied by a slow consumption of the carbon of each. rod.
This flow of electricity produces high
temperature, and intense incandescence
and combustion of the carbon particles.
This is the arc. One lamp differs from
another only in the way in which the carbons are moved forward as they consume,
so as to maintain the resistance equal
and the light steady. Among arc lamps,
that which signaled itself out among all
its compeers, for steadiness and brilliancy, was the Jaspar lamp, exhibited in
the Belgian Section; but it had the disadvantage of absorbing all the energy of
one machine. Among those that admit-
ted of having a number on one section,
perhaps the simplest in its construction
was the Gülcher, exhibited in the Austrian Section; but the most effective and
original was the "Pilsen" lamp, the in-

vention of Messrs. Piette & Krisik. It is
called the "Pilsen" lamp, from the place
of its birth, and from the want of eupho-
niousness in the names of its inventors.
It was exhibited in the Austrian Section,
and also in the British Section, by Mr.
Fyfe. The carbons are kept apart by a
sucking coil when the current flows; they
are regulated by a second sucking coil
worked on a shunt. The peculiarity of
the lamp consists principally in the shape
of the core that controls the carbon—it
is wedge-shaped at each end; in action is
wonderfully regular, and almost perfect.
Six lamps were worked in one circuit by
a Schuckert machine.

The *Lampe Soleil*, which holds an in-
termediate position between arc and incandescent lamps, made a very effective
display in the picture gallery, where there
were 20 lamps in 10 lanterns. It is to
be seen in London lighting up the Pano-
rama in Westminster. It is a fixed,
steady, durable lamp, giving a soft yel-
lowish light, which is due to the fact that
the arc maintains in incandescence a

highly refractory substance like marble, between the two ends at the carbon. It is a very simple lamp, for it involves no mechanism whatever; but it is said to absorb a great deal of power, though I have seen no reliable figures of its performance. Its consumption of carbon is remarkably small. It is worked by an alternate current machine, which, like most of these machines, made a most unpleasant hum.

Carrè made a very fine display of carbons for arc lights, for the manufacture of which he is so famous, in which the regularity of form, of structure, and of composition, is said to be absolute; but it is very questionable whether this is really the case in practice, for the irregularity of the arc lights is chiefly due to impurities and irregularities in the carbon. Moreover, the very vast discrepancies that are found in the photometric measurements of the same lamp at different times, or by different persons, may be due to the irregularities in the structure of the artificial carbon rods.

No one can deny that the Jablockhoff candle has done good service in the cause of electric lighting; but I am afraid that the Exhibition in Paris has sounded the knell of all forms of candle, as well as those of the Werderman type. The rising favorite is the incandescent lamp, pure and simple. The display made by Mr. Swan in the buffet, in the Congress Hall, and in the Pavilion at the Post-office, was brillant and effective. The light was soft, uniform, and yellow. The incandescent light is totally free from those bright rays that are so injurious to the eyes, so uncomplimentary to the complexion, and so irritating to the worker, if they are accompanied with the least unsteadiness. It is so readily under control; it requires no skilled labor to replace it or attend to it; it can be fixed anywhere; it can be worked into the fixtures and decorations of a room, and it does not damage them, as gas and oil do. Incandescent lamps can be worked by either continuous or alternate current machines. In fact, the chief lesson of the Paris Exhibition is this, that the arc light is specially suited for external illumination, and that incandescent lamps are eminently adapted for internal and for domestic illumination. This lesson has been carried into practice at the Savoy Theatre, where nothing can be more effective or more efficient than the illumination of the auditorium. One can breathe pure air, feel cool, and can sit out a play without incurring a headache. There were several incandescent lamps shown at Paris besides those of Mr. Swan, notably those of Maxim and Lane-Fox; but that which possessed the greatest novelty, and was decidedly the most efficient, was that of Mr. Edison. The distinctive character of the Edison lamp is the remarkable uniformity of its texture and light-giving power. The lamp consists of a fine filament of carbon inserted as a part of the electric circuit in a glass globe, which has been exhausted of air to the utmost limit of workshop skill. A fine, uniform quality of Japanese bamboo has been se-

lected as that which gives the finest fila
ment for carbonizing. The bamboo is
cut by special machinery into the required dimensions, and inserted in a
mould, which is placed in a furnace, and
raised to a very high temperature, and
from which the filament comes out
shaped and carbonized. Naturally grown
vegetable fiber has been found to give a
more uniform texture than any artifici-
ally-formed carbon. The ends are cut
flat, and squeezed inside copper clamps,
which are then welded together by
electro-plating. The copper clamps being
soldered to platinum leads that are sealed
through the glass, and are connected to
the conductors. Perfect sealing is obtained by flattening the mass of the tube,
through which the fine platinum wires
pass into a solid bar, so as to well fuse
the wires and glass together. It is a
fortunate thing for the permanence of
the incandescent lamp that the co-efficient
of expansion, due to heat, of glass and
platinum is practically the same.

The normal lamp consists of a filament

6 inches long, which gives a resistance
of 240 ohms when cold, and, when per-
meated by a current of 0.8 ampere, gives
a light equivalent to 16 sperm candles.
The half lamp is constructed with a carbon filament of just half the length and
half the resistance, and gives eight
candles. Other lamps are made with two
and four horse-shoe filaments, so as to
increase the light-giving power. The
features of carbon, which render it so
highly adapted for incandescence, are its
electrical resistance, its high refractory
character, and its stability. The illumination of a filament and its durability are
functions of the current that passes ; the
more intense the current the higher the
temperature, and therefore the brighter
the light and the shorter its life. At a
temperature of about 1,000° carbon becomes red, at 2,000° it is white, and the
higher the temperature the whiter it
gets, until it fuses. A current of 0.8 of
an ampere maintains an Edison filament
at about 2,000°, when it gives a light of
16 candles, and it lasts on an average

1,000 hours. A stronger current will give a much better light, but the carbon will not last so long. If it were possible to find a form of carbon, or any other material, which would be so refractory that we could transmit through it much stronger currents, the incandescent lamp would rival the arc lamp in brilliancy and power.

The destruction of the carbon filament in incandescent lamps is due to what is called the Crookes' effect, a very slow transference of carbon, in a molecular shower, from the one heel to the other heel of the horseshoe, until a breakdown takes place at the former point. The better the vacuum the slower this effect.' Alternate current machines are said to lengthen the life of the carbons, by equalizing the distribution of molecules on each heel, but they do so at the expense of efficiency.

Many devices were shown for measuring the quantity of electricity consumed in any place by electric lamps ; but that adopted by Mr. Edison is sufficiently simple and accurate for all practical purposes. A glass cell contains two copper plates immersed in a solution of sulphate of copper. A definite proportion (0.001) of the current that passes through the house passes also through this cell. and removes copper from one plate and de posits copper on one plate. The weight of copper deposited is an exact measure of the current used. There are two such cells—the one in charge of the consumer and the other of the supplier. They thus check each other.

Various plans were shown in different parts of the Exhibition to diffuse the light, but the most effective was that in *Salle* 15. where a Jaspar lamp filled the room with a shadowless light, by throwing a light on to a white screen above the lamp, whence it was scattered. The lamp itself was invisible. This plan is not novel. It was suggested by the Duke of Sutherland, and has been adopted by Mr. Schwendler in India.

The proper distribution of light is a problem that remains to be solved. It is

argued that an arc is so much superior
to an incandescent light, that one-horse
power in the former gives you ten times
more light than in the latter. This is
true; but, on the other hand, to obtain a
subdued light sufficient for your purpose,
you must either put the arc lamp far
away or tone it down by shades, and
therefore waste it; whereas an incandescent lamp can be toned down, by regulating the current, to any color you like,
and it can be fixed just where it is
wanted. One-horse power will give you
1,500 candles in an arc, and only 160
candles in 10 incandescent lamps; but
these 10 lamps can be so distributed
about your space to be lit, as to illuminate your surface or objects with a better light than the arc.

Curiously enough nothing whatever
was done in Paris to improve the illumination of streets. The Avenue de l'Opera,
the first street practically lighted by
electricity, still remains as it was in 1878;
but prior to the opening of the Exhibition. a portion of the Boulevard des

Italiens was lit up by four De Mersanne lamps, suspended high up, at wide intervals, over the center of the road. The effect was very fine, but the lamps were very bad. This is the true way of illuminating streets, and it is to be regretted that such an experiment is not tried in London. Street illumination in England by electricity up to the present time is, as a rule, a questionable success.

The question remains for discussion: Has the electric light been brought within the region of practical domestics? I have no hesitation in saying that it has: but whether it can be brought into economical contrast with gas, experience alone will show. Several houses are already illuminated by its agency; others are in hand, my own amongst the number; and when we next meet to consider this subject, I may be able to answer the question with actual facts.

One word as regards the danger of electric lighting. There is no use blinking our eyes to the fact that electricity can be a dangerous servant in the hands of the careless and ignorant ; in the hands of the skilled it has less danger than gas, or even oil. The installation of the wires must be controlled by experience and knowledge. I have more than once called attention to this fact, and my warnings have been received with abuse; but in Paris there were no less than five incipient fires, from the wires coming in contact with each other, in the Exhibition building. The *Times* correspondent in Vienna implies that the frightful disaster to the Ring Theatre was due to this cause. The instances in New York are so numerous that the Board of Fire underwriters have issued the following rules : —

" 1. Wires to have 50 per cent. excess of conductivity above the amount calculated as necessary for the number of lights to be supplied by the wire.

" 2. Wires to be thoroughly insulated and doubly coated with some approved material.

" 3. All wires to be securely fastened by some approved non-conducting fastening, and to be placed at least 2½ inches for incandescent light, and 8 inches for arc lights, from each other, and 8 inches from all other wires and from all metal or other conducting substance, and to be placed in a manner to be thoroughly and easily inspected by surveyors. When it becomes necessary to carry wires through partitions and floors, they must be secured against contact with metal or other conducting substance in a manner approved by the inspector of the Board.

"4. All arc lights must be protected by glass globes enclosed at the bottom, to effectually prevent sparks or particles of the carbons from falling from the lamps : and in show windows, mills, and other places where there are materials of· an inflammable nature, chimneys with spark arresters shall be placed at the top of the globe. Open lights positively prohibited. The conducting framework of chandeliers must be insulated and covered the same as wires.

" 5. Where electricity is conducted into a building (from sources other than the building in which it is used) a shut-off must be placed at the point of entrance to each building, and the supply turned off when the lights are not in use. Applications for permission to use electric lights must be accompanied with a statement of the number and kind of lamps to be used, the estimate of some known electrician of the quantity of electricity required. and a sample of the wire (at least three feet in length) to be used, with a certificate of said electrician of the carrying capacity of said wire. The applications should also state where the electricity is to be generated, whether the connection will have metallic or ground circuit, and, as far as possible. give full details of the manner in which it is proposed to equip the building."

These rules are very simple, and are necessarily carried out by every qualified electrician, but an additional security is obtained by Mr. Edison, by inserting in every branch wire a "safety catch," which is a short piece of lead wire that instantly melts if the strength of the current exceeds a certain value, and thus ruptures the circuit, stopping the flow of electricity, and producing safety.

The completeness of Mr. Edison's exhibit was certainly the most noteworthy object in the exhibition. Nothing seems to have been forgotten, no detail missed. There we saw not only the boilers, engine, and dynamo machine, but the pipes to contain the conductors; the conductors themselves, heavy and mass-·ive, for Mr. Edison recognizes the waste of energy that must occur in small conductors, the insulation, the fixtures, the brackets, the safety catches, the lamps, devices to avoid the effects of expansion and contraction through changes of temperature, meters to measure the current used, regulators to control the consumption of fuel. In a properly regulated system there ought to be no waste of fuel. The engine driver has an indicator which shows him exactly what current is going out, and he has simply to regulate his firing by this indicator. Moreover, by the use of a rheostat, he is also able to regulate the outgoing current so that he is able to maintain a perfect ratio between the fuel consumed and the light evolved.

The question that determines the size and insulation of conductors is a commercial one, 'and is regulated by the relative economy of waste of energy or interest on capital expended. If an expenditure of £100 per mile saves you £10 a year in fuel, it is clearly better to expend £100 on your conductor. If, on the other hand, it would save you only £2 a year, it is better to utilize your capital elsewhere. Every inch of conductor means waste of energy; the shorter and heavier it is the less the waste; but as some waste is imperative, it is simply a matter of calculation to determine which shall be wasted least, capital or fuel.

The system is self-regulating, if the electromotive force is kept constant, and the resistance of the lamps be uniform. We have the dynamo machine at one end of the circuit, and a lamp at the other.

The circuit is complete ; a small current flows, which is determined by the resistance of the lamp alone, if the main conductors are made sufficiently large to neglect their resistance. Additions and subtractions of lamps only vary the resistance, and, therefore, the current. Turning off one lamp does not interfere with the rest. The limit of the number of lamps inserted is determined by their resistance and by the heating of the armature ; hence the value of high resistance in the lamps, and low resistance in the armature of the dynamo machine. Every lamp induces, as it were, its own current. We have not a store of electricity which has to be subdivided, but we generate our energy as we want it. This is the promising feature of the system. It is a principle of multiplication, rather than of sub-division, and leads one to anticipate economy in its working. Mr. Edison's system has been worked out in detail, with a thoroughness and a mastery of the subject that can extract nothing but eulogy from his bitterest opponents. Many unkind things have been said of Mr. Edison and his promises ; perhaps no one has been severer in this direction than myself. It is some gratification for me to be able to announce my belief that he has at last solved the problem that he set himself to solve, and to be able to describe to the Society the way in which he has solved it.

It may be taken as a rule, that any system dependent on the exercise of abnormal energy is certain sooner or later to break down ; we all of us hate personal supervision, and personal supervision at home is a species of abnormal energy. This is the great secret of the success of gas. It is the cause of the slow progress of the arc light ; but it is because the incandescent light promises to rival gas in this respect, that such a future is open to it.

The awards at the Paris Exhibition were liberally bestowed by the jury, perhaps too much so ; but matters were hurried up towards the end, owing to

political difficulties, and the conclusions
were necessarily hasty. No proper
measurements or tests were made by
any jury, but a committee, presided over
by M. Tresca, has since been formed to
continue the work, and there is no doubt
that most valuable results will be obtained, for the desire of the jury to pro-
cure reliable measurements has been very
generally met by the exhibitors. I had
great hopes of being able to give you
the results to-night, but the reports are
not yet complete.

We shall all, very soon, have a repe-
tition on a different scale, and in a different way, at the Crystal Palace, and I
have little doubt that. in its way, the
Crystal Palace Exhibition will be as fine
and as interesting as that of Paris.

DISCUSSION.

The Chairman said he could not open
the discussion better than by calling on
Mr. Johnson. the representative of Mr.
Edison.

Mr. Johnson said he did not know that he could supplement what had been so well said by Mr. Preece, so as to add to the interest of the subject, but he should be ready to explain anything which had been left unexplained, and he would also illustrate, further, the use of some of the apparatus. He wished, however, to say that Mr. Edison's system was not merely a system of electric lighting; but the novelty of his system lay in this, that he contemplated the manufacture of electricity on a large scale at a central station, and its universal distribution throughout the entire area of the city where it was established. to be used by uneducated or unscientific people, without the supervision of trained experts in the employment of the company. They proposed to put the electric light into houses in such a simplified form, and with such provisions, as to render supervision entirely unnecessary : to bring the lamps within the care of ordinary house servants, no matter how ignorant they might be; and in such a way that no damage or waste was possible. The electricity thus converted into light might also be converted into power, by means of an electro motor ; and it might be utilized in a variety of ways, such as for ringing bells, &c. The annoyance of maintaining a battery, as well as its expense, had hitherto proved a bar to its general use, but when electricity could be supplied and paid for only as used, to be shown by a meter, an immense deal of work, such as driving sewing machines, &c., would be done by it. There had been a good deal of talk about a regulator, and Mr. Preece had shown that one might be made to maintain an even pressure throughout an entire district lighted from one station, no matter how many lamps were lighted by it. They preferred to have such a regulator with personal supervision, just as gas companies regulated the pressure on their mains as required. rather than employing any automatic device, which was liable to get out of order. [Mr. Johnson here showed how the amount of current could be in-

creased or diminished at will, so that
when fewer lights were in use, the quantity would be diminished accordingly.]
The man in charge of the central station
would regulate the current by a sample
lamp kept alight there. He had been
asked whether the replacement of the
lamps, when used up, was expensive or
difficult. In answer to that, he might
say that in New York, where they were
making arrangements to light up a
central district of a mile square, they
proposed to supply every consumer with
all the lamps he might use, free from
cost, simply charging the cost of the
lamp in the current supplied and paid
for on his meter. The first cost of the
lamps was very small to them, and they
therefore preferred supplying them to
subjecting the consumer to the annoyance of having to purchase them. [Mr.
Johnson here unscrewed a lamp, and
attached another, to show the readiness
with which a change could be effected.]
A question had also been asked him,
whether a single light could be raised or

lowered; and there was a lamp made in which this was provided for, but it was more expensive and complicated, and was not recommended. There were very few cases where such would be required, because you need not leave a light on as in the case of gas, in order to light up when required, as you only had to turn it on, and it lit itself.

Sir HENRY TYLER, K.C.B., moved a vote of thanks to Mr. Preece, but remarked that the paper hardly answered to the title, inasmuch as it was mainly devoted to an explanation of Mr. Edison's lamps, and he thought there might have been a little more time bestowed upon other lamps. He was far from wishing to disparage the Edison lamp, and no one had more sympathy than he had with American inventors; but he would suggest that the title of the paper should be altered when printed.

Mr. E. CROMPTON said he had been much interested in the paper, but he must concur to some extent in Sir H. Tyler's remarks. Many, if not all, of the

merits of the Edison lamp were common
to other incandescent lamps. He, therefore, thought Mr. Swan and Mr. Lane-Fox
ought not to be passed over in silence,
or Mr. Maxim, the other great American
inventor. Mr. Preece had been rather
hard on the arc systems, which he said
had made comparatively little progress ;
but in reply to that, he would ask the
meeting to look at the length and breadth
of England, where, since that time last
year, there had been from 900 to 1,000
installations of the electric light, which,
with the exception of 30 or 40, were all
on the arc system, and, with very few
exceptions, they were all working most
successfully. The incandescent systems
were working equally successfully, but
the whole system was an infant compared
to the arc, and had not yet been worked
on a sufficiently large scale to judge of
its merits. It had hitherto been placed
in circumstances not best suited for it.
The lighting of the Savoy Theater was a
great success, in his opinion, but no one
could say that that vast open space could

not be lit more satisfactorily with arc lights, if good ones, and properly managed. The arc light hitherto had had to struggle with the great difficulty of getting homogeneous carbons; but new manufacturers were setting to work, and he believed the trade of making these carbons would soon become one of the great industries of the country. It required nothing but the enormous demand, now springing up, to produce splendid carbons, which would give a perfectly satisfactory light.

Mr. J. N. SHOOLBRED said he had nothing to add to Mr. Preece's descript on of the Paris Exhibition, but he thought his remarks as to the future sphere of the arc light and the incandescent light respectively should be somewhat modified. He did not think the arc light need be confined merely to large open spaces. It was a question of the enormous difference of mechanical energy ; and a case which recently came under his notice would illustrate this. It was the interior of a building considerably larger than

that hall, which it was found would require about 6-horse power to light it by
the arc system, whilst on the incandescent system it would have taken nearly
40-horse power, and from 170 to 200
lights. With regard to the experiments
shown that evening. he must fully concur
in what had been said as to the beautifully
steady character of the lights, but at the
same time it was only fair that due
credit should be given to other inventors.

Mr. HUGH CLEMENTS remarked that Mr.
Edison had evidently gone beyond any
one else, up to the present time, in the
manufacture of his 20-ton machine at any
rate. Mr. Preece, of course, could not
enter fully into the details of all the
lights; but he understood him now to
withdraw a statement he had made on a
former occasion, that it was impossible
for private houses to be lit up by electricity from a central station. There
was evident proof that this was being
done in New York, and he hoped the
time would soon come when they would
see the same thing in London.

Captain VERNEY, R.N., said it might be interesting to the meeting to hear the opinion of one of the general public, entirely unconnected with any electrical interest. He had visited the Paris Exhibition twenty or thirty times, and had been many times in both the Edison and Swan rooms. He must say that he came away with the impression that on the whole the Lane-Fox was the most satisfactory exhibit. He was also much impressed with the beauty of the *Lampe Soleil*, which Mr. Preece had alluded to, but not described very minutely. One of its great beauties was, that you could introduce other substances as a bridge between the carbons, and thus vary the color and quality of the light. The light was exceedingly soft and agreeable, being generally overhead, and it seemed to him an enormous advantage to be able to introduce marble, magnesium, or some other substance, and so tone the light as to be suitable to the place to be illuminated. He hoped those who had the management of the Exhibition at Crystal

Palace, would enable the general public to gather from it more information than was available at Paris. There they were furnished with an incomprehensible catalogue, referring to numbers which did not exist, and to rooms which could not be found. It was a most perplexing thing for any one with the average amount of intelligence and energy, to learn anything from the Paris Exhibition.

Mr. Lascelles Scott did not propose to launch upon the vexed question with which the discussion opened, further than to suggest that, as Mr. Preece had on former occasions spoken rather adversely to Mr. Edison, he felt constrained now, with more information, to do him full justice. He thought the time was hardly arrived to pronounce definitely that the arc light was only suitable for large open areas, and that the incandescent system was best for internal use, or *vice versa*, because in all probability, in a few years, such an opinion would be very much modified. Judging from his own small experience, he desired to place

on record his opinion that probably the
domestic lamp of the future would be
one in which the prominent features
of both systems were combined, which
would illuminate a room alternately, or
almost at the same time, by either a small
arc or an incandescent lamp. There was
already a system which professed to do
something of the kind.

The CHAIRMAN said he thought that
the last speaker had really given the answer to the objection raised by Sir H.
Tyler, by referring to Mr. Preece's desire to restore the equilibrium of the
balance, which, on a former occasion, had
been unduly depressed on one side.
Passing from this matter and going to
the real subject of the paper, they had
before them a remarkable example of the
incandescent light, and he thought they
must all agree that if this light could be
introduced into houses, in the same way
as gas, and at no greater, or a very little
greater. expense, it would be forthwith
adopted. A lamp which did not vitiate
the atmosphere in the least, which gave

off but a small amount of heat, which
was capable of being absolutely extin-
guished, and then renewed again in a
moment, was one which all would wil-
lingly take instead of a gas lamp, which
certainly did pollute the air, heated it in-
conveniently, and if there were too much
pressure, or the burner were out of order, smoked and spoiled the furniture
and pictures. Under these circumstances
he thought it could not be doubted that
if they could all, by a mere word, change
their gas fittings and lights to such as
they saw there, that word would be ut-
tered; but then came the question, how
near were they to that being practically
and commercially possible? He believed
they were very near to it. It had been
said, and truly, of the electric light, as
one of Dickens' characters said of the
steam engine, that it was yet in its in-
fancy. Sometimes infants grew up well,
and became a pleasure to their parents;
sometimes they grew up ill; but he believed this infant would turn out a credit
to its parents, and that they would soon

have the electric light laid on in the manner which had been stated. The difficulties at present attendant on applying it to individual houses, were those connected with the motive power, a large question which he could not then fully go into: but there was a system, somewhat inaccurately called "storage of electricity," by which there might be brought into any house a number of boxes, not storing electricity, but each containing an apparatus which had, by the agency of electricity, been put into a condition competent to develop electricity in an absolutely regular manner, a most needful quality for the satisfactory production of the incandescent light, although he must say no want of steadiness was observable from the working of the engine that evening. You could, therefore, by the aid of these boxes, practically have electricity brought into your house, as you had gazogenes, ready charged, or as he remembered many years ago, portable gas was carted to houses in this city. Unless there were some such system as that, persons who wanted to use the electric light had to resort to a motor of some kind, and there was the choice between steam engines and gas engines. A large steam engine at present was more economical than a gas engine, but on the other hand, it required a more skilled attendant. To work a gas engine, you had to do little more than turn a tap, and to oil occasionally; the stoker and engine driver were really at the gas works. The manager there supplied a regular flow and pressure of gas, and in that way the labor of attendance to each engine was reduced to a minimum. In the case of small engines, this non-necessity for skilled attendance reduced the cost practically far below that of a steam engine. For that reason, he believed, that the individual lighting of houses would be done by gas engines, and that if you took the gas with which your house was lighted, and applied it to work an engine, you would obtain a greater amount of light from incandescent lamps than by burning the gas direct. The calculation had been gone into very carefully, and were it not for the cost of replacing the lamps, it was quite clear that even now economy was considerably on the side of electricity. He was glad to hear from Mr. Johnson that in America the company preferred to include the replacement of the lamps in the fixed charge for the electricity; but that could hardly be done where each man had to produce his own electric current. A thousand hours was stated to be the average life of these lamps, some being much above and others much below the average. The other day a committee, of which he was a member, did not feel it safe to calculate the average at more than 500 hours, and then putting the cost of renewal at 5s., it turned out that that, added to the fuel, made the electric lighting rather dearer than gas, and they had deferred the consideration of the matter for a few weeks to obtain further information. But if electricity could be laid on to houses, no doubt the problem would be, to a large extent, solved. One of the great difficulties was in the meter, but they had had one of a very ingenious and apparently efficient character exhibited that evening, and that might render practicable the establishment of a company for laying on electricity like gas or water, charging the consumer only for what he used. With regard to another point which had been considered a great difficulty—the division of the current—Mr. Preece said it was not really a divided current, but that each lamp induced its own current. That did not seem to him a very happy mode of expressing it, and he would endeavor to explain it in another way. Each of the lamps they would see, was situated between two parallel wires, from which went two small wires, which were attached to the filament of carbon in the lamp. Now, if instead of electricity they supposed water were being used, and that the wires represented the pipes, and one pipe contained a pressure of water, while the other acted as a return pipe, there being no connection between the two except by small pipes, represented by the wires going to each lamp, as long as only one of these small pipes was opened, the quantity which would pass would be only as much as could be transmitted by the one small connecting pipe ; if two were opened, there would be double the quantity, and so on. Assuming for the moment that none of the pipes were open, then having once established a pressure of water, it required no energy to maintain it, if there were no leaks. You could bring the pressure np to a 100 lbs. on the square inch, and if there were no leak it would continue for ever ; but if you established a connection between the pressure pipe and the return pipe, and allowed one gallon per minute to flow away, you must exert as much energy as would supply one gallon per minute under a pressure of 100 lbs. Similarly, if you established a connection between one wire and another, which allowed a given amount of electricity to pass, you must employ as much energy as would develop electricity equal in quantity and ten-

sion to that which had passed away:
if you had ten wires connected,
you must develop ten times as much
energy. So that it was not in truth
a sub-division of the current, but was allowing the current to flow, and regulating the amount of power to be put on
accordingly. It would be easy to ascer-
tain, by an indicator at the central station, what the demands were, and determine what should be the amount of
pressure, as it were, in the conductors,
and the number of horse power required
to be developed in the engine, in order
to supply the pressure. Mr. Johnson
gave as an illustration the governor at a
gas works, which controlled the pressure
in the mains, and which had to be varied,
from time to time, according to the draft
upon them. At this time of the year,
probably at half-past three, there would
be a rise of pressure of so many tenths,
another rise at four, again at half-past
four, and so on until you got to the time
when the theaters and shops were all
using gas ; and then came the maximum,

which would be maintained until ten, when there would be a slight reduction, and a further reduction at midnight, when the uniform night pressure would come on and be maintained until about . six; and then perhaps the day pressure would come on. and be maintained until the afternoon. A gas manager plotted this out on a sheet of paper which was affixed to the instrument, and this drew on the same sheet of paper, a trace showing the amounts and the durations of the pressure actually given, by the governors, so that, according to the way in which the pencil followed the lines already laid down, the manager could judge of how his directions had been carried out. Thus, by looking at the paper, you could tell if there had been a foggy day. If the day pressure provided for was say $\frac{12}{10}$, and the implement showed there had been $\frac{20}{10}$, you would know that there had been a fog, that the paper had had to be disregarded, and extra pressure put on. As he understood, provision would be made in the same way for

increasing the electric current when required. With respect to the arc and in.
candescent lights, they would all agree
that no one could dogmatize on what
would be the light of the future, the
whole matter being, as yet. too much in
the trial stage; but, at present, he thought
all would prefer the incandescent light
for domestic illumination. It was ad-
mitted that the arc light was much more
economical, perhaps 10 to 1; Mr. Shoolbred said 8 to 1. Then Mr. Preece ob-
jected to the arc light being placed high
up; but it was shown conclusively to the
committee that sat on the lighting of
Liverpool, that there really was no loss
by placing the light high up. It was
true the .effect of the light diminished
with the square of the distance, and that,
therefore, a light a hundred feet up
would give only one - hundredth. part
of the intensity of light that would
be given by the same light if it were
ten feet up; but, assuming an equal
diverging angle for the really effective
rays, it would, on the other hand,

light a hundred times the area. The only difference, probably, would be the want of penetrating power in case of fogs.

The vote of thanks having been passed unanimously,

Mr. PREECE, in reply, said it appeared that his sins had been rather of omission than commission, and this would be further explained by the opening paragraphs of his paper. It must also be remembered that that was the third or fourth time he had read a paper before the So. ciety on electric lighting, and the sixth or seventh time he had spoken on the subject, and he had not, of course, again gone over ground he had already trodden. It would not be true to entitle his paper a description of the Edison light, as other matters were treated; but it was evident that what he had said abou it, and what had been seen by the audience, had produced a very deep impression on their minds.